THE Love PLAYBOOK

THE *Love* PLAYBOOK

RULES FOR LOVE, SEX, AND HAPPINESS

LA LA ANTHONY

WITH KAREN HUNTER

A CELEBRA BOOK

Celebra
Published by the Penguin Group
Penguin Group (USA) LLC, 375 Hudson Street,
New York, New York 10014

USA | Canada | UK | Ireland | Australia | New Zealand | India | South Africa | China
penguin.com
A Penguin Random House Company

First published by Celebra,
a division of Penguin Group (USA) LLC

First Printing, February 2014

LIBRARY OF CONGRESS CATALOGING-IN-PUBLICATION DATA:
Anthony, La La.
The love playbook: rules for love, sex, and happiness/La La Anthony, with Karen Hunter.
p.   cm.
ISBN 978-0-451-46644-0
1. Man-woman relationships.   2. Sex.   3. Happiness.
4. Anthony, La La.   I. Hunter, Karen.   II. Title.
HQ801.A64 2014
306.7—dc23   2013037847

Printed in the United States of America
10   9   8   7   6   5

Set in Garamond

PUBLISHER'S NOTE
While the author has made every effort to provide accurate telephone numbers and Internet
addresses at the time of publication, neither the publisher nor the author assumes any
responsibility for errors, or for changes that occur after publication. Further, publisher does
not have any control over and does not assume any responsibility for author or third-party
Web sites or their content.

To my grandmother, Celina Surillo (Mami Nina).

I hold you in my heart every day.

CONTENTS

Contents

Contents

OPENING TIP
I'm **Not** a Relationship Expert, but . . .

"I don't like to play games." I hear a lot of people say this as it relates to their relationships. And what I say to that is if you aren't playing, you're probably being played.

I've learned over the years that love and life are one big game. If you want to win, first you have to play (you gotta be in it to win it, as they say, right?). Once you're in the game, then you need to know the rules. The first rule of love is that the ball is in the woman's court.

Most women don't know this and that's why they don't play very well. Imagine giving away your biggest advantage by tossing the ball to him first!

Women control the game. We are the trophy; we have what men want.

I was talking with a couple of male friends one evening recently—regular guys, not athletes or rappers or actors—and they were saying how they hate going to clubs to meet women. Why? Because if they see a woman they may like and want to buy her a drink, they usually have to make the first move. Or if they want to dance with a woman they see across the room, they have to walk across the room and ask her to dance. They talked about the anxiety of that walk. They talked about their fear of rejection. All the things they worried about were things that the woman on the other side of the room doesn't even have to consider.

> The first rule of love is that the ball is in the woman's court.

She holds the power. If she says no, he has to handle that and figure out what his next move is going to be. These guys are good-looking, have great jobs, and are confident and secure in themselves, so it was surprising to hear how scared they were to approach a woman.

It made me remember, too, that I experienced this myself when I was in high school. I was popular, I was cool, and I was dateless. I hung with all the guys (many of whom I'm still friends with), but none of them asked me to the prom or even on a date. They thought that either I was taken or there was no way they had a chance—not because I was some supermodel knockout but because I was so confident-seeming and cool that I probably would say no. I never got the chance to say no. So I eventually learned that it was okay to make the first move (more on this later).

There are a lot of good men out there looking for a relationship—not just a hookup. For those guys looking just for a hookup, it's a numbers game: Ask as many women as possible or date as many women as possible and if you get one, great. That's probably not what you're looking for, and you can see this dude a mile away. He's the one with the smooth lines, and he seems to have it all figured out and knows exactly what you like.

But a man who is serious, who wants to settle down, who is looking for *that woman*—he's not thinking that way. If you're a woman looking for a guy like that, then know that you totally have the upper hand. Once you know that you control the game, the next thing you must know is what the rules are.

Here's another often unknown fact: Women usually make the rules. We determine a lot of how our relationships will play out by the decisions we make or don't make early on. We determine how a man will treat us. We determine how *far* things will go and *how* they will go. Depending on what kind of outcome you want, you can set your rules accordingly.

Being married to an NCAA basketball champion and

two-time Olympic gold medalist who is one of the best players in the NBA, I get to see what it takes to win a game, a series, and a championship. There's a lot of preparation, conditioning, and training—and that's before the season even starts. During the season they still have to work out and practice. They watch tapes of other teams to study weaknesses and figure out how to exploit them. It's not enough that their team is good; they have to find ways to beat that other team, which is also very good. Even with the best conditioning, training, coaching, and facilities, they still need teamwork and a bit of luck to win.

There are a lot of similarities between the game of basketball (and most games) and the game of love. In both basketball and love, if you want to win, you have to work hard and you need teamwork. But in basketball, there can be only one winner. In love, if you play the game right, you both win.

Too many women, however, play to lose.

How do we lose?

1. We don't view other women as members of our team. As women, we spend too much time competing with one another, being catty, talking trash about one another, and being disloyal to one another. That gives men a tremendous advantage. Divide and conquer. Men today can pretty much get away with whatever they want to in a relationship because women are so busy tearing one another down they lose sight of the game itself. Not only do we

betray one another far too often, but we also betray ourselves by allowing men to get away with certain things.

2. We don't set the standard for how we expect to be treated. We leave it up to the men to figure out. I believe I heard someone say on *Oprah* (maybe it was Dr. Phil) that you teach people how to treat you. The reason why so many women are in an unhappy relationship, or no relationship at all, is that they haven't set a standard for how they expect to be treated—mostly because they haven't yet figured out how they want to be treated or how they deserve to be treated. You have to know yourself (and if you don't, work on finding out who you are) and know what you want in your relationship.

I'm not saying you should have this ridiculous laundry list of dos and don'ts and deal breakers, etc., but you should establish that you're worthy of respect and that you expect to be treated with respect. It's been my experience that men respect women who respect themselves.

3. We make the game far too easy. We fall in love and we just give it all away at once. Men are competitive. Men are hunters. They love a challenge. Why do we take away the hunt by serving the meat on a pretty plate, all seasoned and cooked and even cut into neat little pieces for them? Most women today give it all away and leave nothing for a man to work for or look forward to.

These are just some of things I've learned over the years.

But let me be clear: I am *not* a relationship expert.

I know people look at my life and they think I have it all together and all figured out and that I have everything a woman could want. I have a husband, a beautiful son, money, a career, but . . . my life is not perfect. I don't have all the answers. I wish someone would tell *me* how to keep my shit on track sometimes. But I am that chick that all my friends—and even a few strangers—turn to for advice. It's been that way since I was young, and it has followed me through adulthood. Even some of my male friends call me from time to time to get my take on what's going on in their relationships.

I'm told that I give really good advice. It's easy to look at a situation from the outside and tell someone what you think. But it's *how* I give advice that I think people really appreciate. I have been on the other side of the fence, *getting* advice, and have had people make me feel like crap after I've shared something very personal in my life.

When I made a fool of myself with my first real boyfriend, there were a couple of family members who just shook their heads and gave me that "I told you so . . ." look. My dad, however, didn't ask any questions, didn't make any foul comments. When I called him to come get me and take me away from the situation, he was there unconditionally. He let me cry, and he made me feel like it would all be okay. I already felt like crap; I didn't need to hear about how stupid I was on top of it.

I knew I never wanted to make someone feel bad about a choice they'd made or were thinking about making. Even if I thought their situation was crazy and even if they decided not to listen to my advice and did something that ended up blowing up in their face, I would never say "I told you so," and I definitely wouldn't make them feel bad, no matter what they decided to do or not do.

We all make mistakes, nobody is perfect, and shit happens.

Once that's established, let's try to figure out how to get through it and how to make sure you don't keep making the same mistakes over and over again.

My mother used to always tell me that it's better to learn from others' mistakes than to learn the hard way by making the mistakes on your own. She couldn't have been more right, and that is why I'm writing this book.

I'm writing the book I wish I had had when I was first dating or when I got my heart broken. I wish someone had written a book telling me how he or she got over someone they never thought they would get over. I wish there had been a book where I could hear from someone my age who had been through some of the things I was going through and am going through, just to feel like I'm not alone or crazy.

This is that book.

I will share my experiences, some stories from my friends, and some of the things I've learned from people like my mom, grandmother, father, and stepfather about love and relationships.

Among my close friends, we have this saying: "No judgment." No matter what we share, no matter what we've done, there is no judgment. It is so liberating to have a group of girlfriends that I can share things with, and vice versa. We all truly have one another's backs. I cannot stress enough how important it is to have good friends. But before you deserve to have good friends, you have to *be* a good friend.

I try to be a great friend, always.

Not only is there no judgment among me and my friends, but there's also a lot of understanding, compassion, and love. I depend on my friends to keep me humble and tell me what I need to hear, not necessarily what I want to hear. And I'm that kind of friend to them.

I'm that chick who wants everyone around me to have his or her best possible life. I hate to see people unfulfilled or unhappy. If I can help you in any way, I will. I decided to write this book because I've been asked probably a million times what's the secret to having a successful relationship, how do you make him say "I do," and how do you snag a baller (yes, I get asked that one the most lately).

I have answers to all of those questions, and some may surprise you. I will also help you figure out what to wear on a first date, when you should sleep with him (if at all), and what you can do if you find out he's been cheating.

But more than any of those things, I will share with you the wisdom that has helped me figure some things out along the way.

The best piece of advice I've gotten from my dad is to live your life inside out. Don't worry about what people are saying about you or what someone else thinks. You have to live your life doing what pleases and completes you. And only you can make that happen.

I didn't always take my dad's advice. For a good portion of my life I really did care too much what people thought. I wanted everyone to like me. And having that kind of mentality can make you do a lot of things you wouldn't ordinarily do. It took a few heartbreaks and some hurt feelings for me to decide that my best approach to life is to be true to myself, always.

As long as I have my family and my friends and they love me, nothing else can touch me. You're going to have some wins and some losses, and you're going to make a whole bunch of mistakes, but isn't that what life is all about? Making mistakes, and learning from them?

TIMEOUT

....

Why This Playbook

> **Timeout:** *A halt in the play. This allows the coaches of either team to communicate with the team, e.g., to determine strategy or inspire morale. Timeouts are critical components of the game and can be the difference between winning and losing.*

I want to spend the first few chapters of this book introducing you to my life and my story. While I may be on television a lot, hosting reunions and being on talk shows, many of the things I'm going to share are things I have never talked about publicly. To give my life and relationship advice some context, I thought it was important for you to see what I've been through in my life—the mistakes I've made and the things I've overcome.

All of my experiences have given me tools to find success in life and love. I have also seen a lot through the experiences of my friends. Hopefully, some of these lessons that I'm sharing with you can help you find your path as well.

CHAPTER ONE

The Daddy Give-and-Go

Give-and-go: A very basic play where after passing to a teammate, the passer quickly cuts toward the basket and receives the return pass back from his teammate for the layup.

How a woman relates to a man in relationships depends on her relationship with her father. I really do believe this. For me, I had the benefit of being raised by two very different men, from whom I was able to learn a lot not just about men but also about what I wanted for myself.

My parents split up when I was about seven years old. I was so young that I don't remember my dad being in the house with us often. The primary reason why my parents split was because my father was never home. He never settled down. He was, and still is, what they call a free spirit. This was great for my mom, she told me, when they were dating and when they first got married. It was all fun and games, partying and freedom. But when they had kids, my mother felt that all of that needed to stop. My dad didn't.

He got a job as a flight attendant that took him all over the world. He would call my mom during a layover in Paris and tell her he was staying for a few days to hang out with friends. My dad is a social butterfly. He loves people and makes friends easily. I'm a lot like him in that way. By the end of his first year as a flight attendant he had friends all over the world and was determined to visit them every chance he got.

He would be in Paris one week, England the next, Switzerland another week. He was having the time of his life, while my mother was left with the responsibility of taking care of the home and my younger brother and me. And she had a full-time job, working at Brooklyn Hospital. She figured since she was basically doing it all alone, she might as well make it official, and she left him.

I never resented my dad for being who he is, for living his truth. To this day, no one can say a bad word about my dad. I love him to pieces. Choosing to live his life the way he did didn't make him a bad person or even a bad dad. It made him adventurous. He is who he is, and I always accepted that.

And he never ran away from his responsibilities to us.

He always paid his child support—never missed a payment. He was also there whenever we needed him.

I guess I didn't miss him as much when he was traveling because we had so much family around us. My uncles, my grandparents—they all filled in whatever blanks we might have had with my dad not being around.

A few years after my mom and dad split up, my mom introduced us to a man I'll call John. He was a nice man. I know now he was a good man. But he wasn't my father.

They had a whirlwind romance, and before we knew it they were getting serious.

My mother and John took my brother and me to Friendly's and announced that they were getting married. I lost it. I went into hysterics. I crawled under the table and cried at the top of my lungs.

They got married anyway, despite my strong reaction, and made it official shortly after at the courthouse. And we were whisked off to Jersey. Culture shock.

We went from the gritty streets of Brooklyn with my very Puerto Rican uncles and grandparents to the bucolic manicured lawns and white picket fences of Piscataway, New Jersey. I was miserable. But it was probably the best thing that could have happened to my life at that time. It both helped me know myself—what I liked and what I didn't like—and gave me the kind of boundaries and restrictions that had me figuring out how in the world I would break free. Because I was determined to break free.

I refused to accept John. He was not our dad—something I reminded him of every chance I got. He was our anti-dad. John had a corporate job. He was an accountant, which I thought was totally boring. He was going to his office every day, while my dad was sending us pictures of himself in front of Buckingham Palace with the queen's guards. Totally cool.

But John made good money and he was able to provide a good life for us. And my mother loved him. She also knew what she wanted for us, and that meant having a male figure in our lives who was stable and would always be there for us. He was also the kind of man who set boundaries and was big on children having discipline and structure.

My stepfather was a very strict man. He had all of these rules. Like when the phone rang, we were to answer, "Jones residence." *Who says that?* I couldn't hang out after school until all my homework was done, until I watched the six o'clock news and read several chapters from whatever book he assigned to us and completed the pages in a workbook associated with that book. By the time I finished all that, I had no time for hanging out with my friends! He was a stickler for education. He wanted us to know everything that was going on in the world, and he would even quiz us from time to time.

My mom certainly wanted us to do well in school, but with my stepfather there were no options. He wasn't mean or abusive or anything. I don't even remember him punishing us. But we just knew what he said was law. I wasn't a particularly rebellious kid (at first), so I went along with whatever he asked. I hated doing it, but I did it anyway. As I got older, I started to really resent it. I felt like I was in jail. And that there was always a deal being made. I couldn't just be a kid and have fun. My fun was always tied to something. I could go and play, but first I had to watch the news. I could go to the movies, but not before I did these pages in a workbook.

I was miserable, and my mom knew it. Well, I wouldn't shut up about it. So she started lying to my stepfather and sneaking behind his back to let me do things. She would tell him I had a doctor's appointment and would drop me off at the mall or the movies for a couple of hours to hang out with my friends. When he would leave for work or if he came home late, I got to watch whatever I wanted on TV. He monitored everything we watched. I even got to stay up later than he allowed. My mom would do things like that often to try and make me happy. This was her way of keeping the peace.

He seemed so unreasonable to me back then.

When the junior prom rolled around, all of my friends got together and their parents rented a stretch limo. I wasn't allowed to ride in the limo with my friends. I was furious.

But I have grown to appreciate the discipline and focus he introduced into my life. I did so well in school that I had many options when it came time for college. I even had a couple of scholarship offers. He also encouraged my love of sports. He was a basketball fanatic, and I got involved in playing and watching basketball with him. I played basketball in junior high and high school because of him. That was one area where we saw eye to eye.

He also sat me down and told me never to date a ball-player. *Never.* I was thirteen and wasn't thinking about dating anyone at the time, but I kept that advice in the back of my mind throughout my teens. In fact, Carmelo didn't stand a chance initially because when I met him all I could think about was my stepfather's warning: "All ball-players are dogs and they only want one thing!"

My mom loved that man, and my brother grew to love him, too. For some reason, I just never warmed up to John. Eventually, our tension became too much for my mother. She was living a double life trying to keep her husband happy and her child happy. The fights between my stepdad and me started to escalate, with me getting bolder and bolder in expressing my disapproval of his rules. I started mouthing off and being disrespectful, and my mom was caught in the middle. When she was faced with a choice between her child and her man, my mom chose me. They were married for about six years and I was sixteen when we left.

We had a comfortable life with our stepfather. We

didn't want for any material thing. But our mom decided that there was something more important than money. That's another lesson I learned from her: There is no amount of money that can replace peace and happiness or your family.

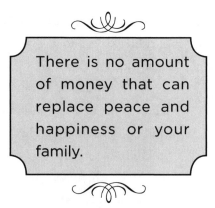

There is no amount of money that can replace peace and happiness or your family.

We moved from a big house in the New Jersey suburbs to a cramped town house with my aunt Edna (Titi Edna) and my cousin Dice in Atlanta. And I couldn't have been happier. Titi Edna was fabulous. She loved to dress and decorate and was very over-the-top. And I loved living there, especially because of Dice. She was the sister I'd never had.

Looking back, I can appreciate the life I had with John. I know I wouldn't be the woman I am today without him. He taught me discipline; he forced me to know more than I ever wanted to know about what was going on in the world. While my dad was traveling the world, John was forcing me to learn about these places. He would have the map out and would test me. I needed to know where Turkey and Bora-Bora and places like that were on the map in relation to where we were. And watching the news every night kept me abreast of what was happening in the world.

That knowledge base came in handy when I was a young girl breaking into TV and radio. I had a depth that not many kids my age had.

I can also thank John for my love of basketball. He allowed me to feel comfortable exploring being an athlete and a bit of a tomboy. He empowered me in that way. I got comfortable in my own skin because there was a man in my home who made me more than okay with that.

I had two men who gave me that sense of confidence. John did it one way. My dad did it in another way with his example of living freely. He gave me another kind of confidence that I could, that I *must*, try anything I wanted to put my mind to.

If my dad weren't the man he is, I probably would not be the woman I am. My dad allowed me to dream and see the big picture and understand that life is about getting out there and living. He lives his life in a way that's very free. I don't think I have ever seen him sad or depressed.

My mom says it's easy to be happy all the time when you don't have any responsibilities. And I hear her. But I think it's more than that for my dad. He sees life in a much different way. And it has helped me to not accept less in my life. It has helped me to pursue my dreams and goals— and to dream big for myself in the first place. And it has also helped me to demand that any man I'm with must honor and respect who I am and what I want to do. This took me just a minute to actually live out, but the seeds of this kind of independence were planted by my dad a long time ago.

I looked at my dad's life as something I wanted to pattern my life after. He lives in Sarasota, Florida, but he really lives wherever he is at that moment. We didn't visit him often, but when we did, all I remember was how small his apartment was and that it wasn't super lived-in. He always seemed to be living out of his luggage. He was either packed to go somewhere, or unpacking from his latest trip. So we never stayed long. Most of the time we would see him when he was on a layover in New York or Newark and later when we moved to Atlanta. We would have him for a couple of hours and we would go to a restaurant and he would fill us in on all the exotic and wonderful places he had visited. I thought that was so cool.

The men who raised me taught me about what I could expect from men in my future. I got to see two very different men who both loved me and wanted the best for me and showed me that they could do that in very different ways. I didn't appreciate my stepfather then. But I do now. My stepfather was all about boundaries and rules. My father was all about freedom and exploration. And I value both.

I also am grateful to my mother for selecting these two men. Women need to be very careful about the men they choose to be with as it pertains to their children. When you're considering being with a man and you want to eventually have children or you are bringing children into the relationship, whether that man is fatherhood material or how that man relates to your children is probably more important than how he relates to you.

This is so important, especially for little girls. Because Daddy will be the first relationship she has with a man—it will shape every relationship she has with every man who comes after.

CHAPTER TWO

The Assist:
Lessons from Mom and Mami Nina

Assist: *The last pass to a teammate that leads directly to a field goal; the scorer must move immediately toward the basket for the passer to be credited with an assist; only one assist can be credited per field goal.*

I believe that many of us model our relationships on what we've seen our mothers or other women do in our lives. Either we do exactly the same thing and end up in the same kinds of relationships, or we watch the hell our mothers, aunts, and grandmothers went through and vow never to let a man do x, y, or z to us.

Often we still end up going through some of the same drama no matter what.

Just as I had two different kinds of male role models, I also had two very different female role models. The first, of course, was my mother. She was the kind of woman who would put up with some hardships, put on a good face for a while, keep things to herself, make a plan. Then she'd bounce.

With my dad, he was perfect until they had kids. My mom, who had a full-time job, understood that she needed a partner who had the time to also be a parent. She wanted a man who would be there day in and day out, not traveling all over the world. So she packed up her kids and left. When she felt that the environment with my stepfather was getting unhealthy for her kids (mostly me), she packed us up and left. She didn't have anything to fall back on—not a job or money—but she knew it was more important that we had a healthy environment than material things.

We went from having just about everything we needed, including a great home, neighborhood, and school, to starting over.

We moved to Atlanta and moved in with my aunt, Titi Edna, who had a small town house. Her home was fiercely decorated with high-end furniture and knickknacks. If you look up the word "diva," that's my Titi Edna, minus the attitude. She loves nice things, jewelry, clothes. It's kind of ironic that Dice is her daughter. My aunt is the epitome of glamour, while Dice is more comfortable in baggy jeans and a sweatshirt.

We invaded their space when we moved to Atlanta, and they welcomed us with open arms. I shared Dice's room, which was small and had only one bed. Dice is an only child and it's unusual for an only child to just be so open to sharing. I was moving in on her territory, sharing her bed, sharing her closet. And she didn't hesitate to make me feel at home.

Dice, who is a year younger than me, also helped me settle in to the new neighborhood and the new school. She was popular and an athlete. The very first day, she took me around and introduced me to everybody. So I wasn't that strange new kid. When school rolled around, we went to school together. We would blast our music in the morning and get ready together. Mark, one of the first people I met when I moved to the neighborhood, would pick us up and drive us to school. He had a red Camaro. His family had money (they owned a restaurant). It was great going to school in style with my buddy. Dice made what could have been a scary and difficult transition so easy and fun.

It was the same with Titi Edna and my mother. They, too, have this unbreakable bond. Titi Edna is older, and when they were growing up she was my mother's protector and best friend. If kids picked on my mother, Titi Edna would be there to beat up those kids—boys or girls. Titi Edna was that bridge for my mom when we moved to

Atlanta until she got on her feet, which she eventually did. She found a good job at the local hospital, and we were able to move to our own apartment at LakePoint, right across the street.

My mom didn't leave my stepfather just because of the tension between John and me. She also left because she wasn't able to be her true self around him. She loved him, but she held back a lot around him, especially when it came to her family, whom she didn't spend as much time with as she'd like when she was with John.

When my uncles would visit our house in New Jersey, my mother would be on pins and needles. Her brothers are very Puerto Rican. They drink hard, they smoke, they talk loud, they love to have fun. And they speak their minds. My mom would always be worried that John would judge them or say something that would create a whole dramatic situation. So she didn't have her family over much while she was married to him.

I learned a lot about relationships from my mom during their breakup. I saw firsthand that if you can't be yourself with a man, you can't be with that man. If he can't accept you—and that means accepting your family, your kids (if you have them), and your dreams—he can't be a part of your life. I also learned that you can't be afraid to leave a bad situation and start over. Or maybe you can be afraid, but don't let your fear stop you. I know my mom had to be afraid to leave the stability and financial comfort of her marriage without a job. But she had people who had her back. I also learned that you need a safety net. For my mom, it was her sister Edna, and the rest of her family. She knew as long as they were there for her, she'd be fine.

The other woman who had a huge influence on me and how I developed in my relationships was my grandmother, my mom's mom. My Mami Nina. She had such a powerful impact on my life. She was

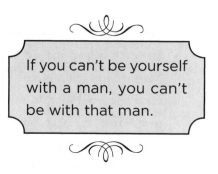

If you can't be yourself with a man, you can't be with that man.

humble and loving. She was the kind of person who tried to help everyone and would give you her last dime if you needed it.

You could come into her house off the streets, filthy, and she would say, "Are you hungry?" And she'd fix you a plate. She never judged. Not even her own kids.

If any of my uncles had an issue, Mami Nina would always be there with a hug and a kind word. You would never know about any problems because she never treated them as if anything was wrong. She had everyone's back.

When I was fourteen, I had long, beautiful hair and I decided to just hack it off. I wanted it to look like Cyndi Lauper's. I came to my grandmother nearly in tears.

"My mom's going to kill me!" I said.

She looked at me and my edgy 'do, and told me to sit.

She did some kind of braid and somehow made it look good. When my mom came home, Mami Nina said, "Look how pretty her hair looks. We tried something different. Don't you like it?" and she winked at me.

She had my mother convinced that my new 'do was nice. My grandmother turned it around and made it okay. She even helped me see my stepfather in a different way. Mami Nina really loved him, and she explained that it takes a special man to raise two children that aren't his own. He didn't have any kids and he took us in and gave us everything we needed.

At the time, I couldn't stand all of his rules. Mami Nina would say, "He's just making sure you're prepared for the real world. He wants you to be successful."

She had so much compassion and understanding.

Mami Nina taught me how to roll with the punches—something I'm still learning. She was from the old school, where you stayed with your man no matter what. My grandfather had his crazy ways, and they even slept in different bedrooms, but my grandmother was there for the long haul. No matter how hectic things might have been, she always had a smile and a sunny disposition. You would never know if she was going through any kind of drama. And I know she had to be. But her attitude was always the same—loving.

I have never come across another human being with a heart like hers.

When I was fifteen, my grandmother got very sick. She and my grandfather had just moved to Atlanta, near my Titi Edna. She was loving the slower pace of the South. We were still in Jersey when they moved from Brooklyn, but I would visit often.

My grandmother was diagnosed with cancer a couple of years after moving to Atlanta. Some of us in the family believe that she knew before she moved from Brooklyn. That's still up for debate. But the cancer spread pretty quickly and she died before my mom, brother, and I moved to Atlanta, too.

In her last days she must have known her time was coming near. She called us all into her hospital room individually to say good-bye. I told her if she died, I was going with her. They would have to admit me into the psych ward because I just knew I would lose my mind.

"No, you're not," she said gently. "You're going to carry on and do all of the great things I see you doing."

Before she died, she told my mother not to put too many reins on me.

"That there is a bird. Let her fly. Don't clip her wings."

Mami Nina knew me even more than I knew myself.

And before she passed she told me, "I will always be with you. If you see a feather anywhere, that's me."

After she died, I would see feathers in the strangest places. I would be having a bad day and I'd be walking along and there would be a feather on the sidewalk. Just lying right there on the sidewalk. Or I could be having a great day and I'd be in a taxi or a car going somewhere and on the seat next to me would be a feather. There would be no birds or pillows or anything around and no other feathers. Just that one feather.

I used to collect them. Now I just smile and say, "Hey, Ma! I see you."

I have a feather tattooed on my hand to remind me that she's always there watching me. It keeps me focused and on the right path by serving as a reminder that I always want to make her proud.

She raised six kids in the Marcy Projects in Brooklyn. I'm sure she never imagined having a child or grandchild grow up to be on TV. They barely had a television in the house.

Whenever I would come to Mami Nina with an issue I was having with someone, from my mother or my step-father to friends or a cousin, she would say, "You have to love people where they are." She told me I had to find something about them that I could love and try to see me in them. If I could find something about them that was like me, then I could love them and not try to change them.

We are all made for a unique purpose and we must all find out what that is for ourselves. And we need to remember that everyone is walking their own path, dealing with their own issues, and trying to find their own happiness.

The best we can do is to appreciate other people for who they are. I learned from Mami Nina the following piece of wisdom, and I've held on to it over the years since she passed: Don't try to change anyone and don't allow anyone to change you.

My mom was the first woman I had a strong relationship with, and to this day, she's one of my best friends. I look to her for reasonable advice.

When I come to my mom, I know she's going to give me commonsense advice that's hard to come by today. Her advice is classic and hasn't been changed by the entertainment industry. She couldn't give a damn about a celebrity. One of the biggest things she would tell my brother and me was to treat people the way we want to be treated. I know it's not a new concept, but she drilled that into us. Her big question would be, "How would you feel if someone did that to you?"

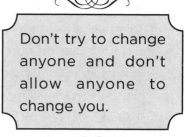

Don't try to change anyone and don't allow anyone to change you.

She wanted you to feel it from that person's perspective. I mean really feel it. And it was effective. I live by that to this day.

My mother was raised in the Marcy Projects in Brooklyn, along with her five brothers and sisters. My grandmother came from Puerto Rico pregnant with Titi Edna. They didn't have any money, but they were as happy as people living in Bel Air. As long as they were together, they were good. My family is close.

I grew up very Hispanic. Three Kings Day. Spanish music, Celia Cruz, Tito Puente. Always, all day long. Spanish food. Rice and beans or *arroz con pollo*. Every day.

My family taught me what is really important in life: family and love.

As a result, I have very high expectations for how a family should relate to one another. It's really hard for me to understand when people don't speak to their mom or they don't get along with their family.

I remember the first time I heard someone say, "Fuck that bitch," referring to his or her mother. I just could never fathom speaking to my mom or about my mom that way. I think it will be really hard to have a great relationship with your man if you can't get right with the people who brought you into this world.

I come from a divorced household, so I'm not saying that you need to see a healthy relationship in your immediate life. You just have to see it somewhere. And more important than that, you need to see what love looks like. That usually starts with the love you have for your mother and/or father.

Whenever I've dated a guy and we've gotten serious, I wanted to have that bond with his family that I had with mine. I realize that perhaps my family is unique and not everyone has that bond. That's fine, just as long as he doesn't allow the dysfunction to creep over into our relationship. We are creatures of habit. If we're used to something since childhood, it's very likely that we will continue those habits and patterns in every relationship we have. He has to be willing to break those patterns and create new ones. But if he's not willing to work through it, you will probably have to let him go. You can't fix a messy relationship unless *he* brings the mop and broom to clean up the mess.

When I've encountered a man who has had a bad relationship with his family, I invite him into mine. I've found over the years that my friends gravitate toward my family. They even ask my mom for advice. That makes me happy because everyone needs to feel like they belong to a family, and if my man can get that through me, it's great. I would rather him have a relationship with his own family, but if he doesn't, he can have one with mine.

I think it's important to look at how a man treats his mom as well. It will determine how he will treat you. It's not absolute, but there is some truth to it. It's not on purpose or malicious, but how can a man really know how to treat you or respect you if he hasn't first done so with his mother? How can you know something you've never been taught?

We can all overcome our upbringing and our tendencies with some hard work, but some people use their dysfunctional or difficult upbringing as an excuse for being fucked up. Don't fall for that game! If he's a grown man, he knows right from wrong. Not having a great upbringing is no excuse for being a jerk. Work on yourself!

If your man is on that pity party train of "my parents were messed up and that's why I'm messed up," run. You're not Iyanla Vanzant. You can't fix his life. He's the only one who can do that. Tell him to call you once he's fixed himself. You can be there for him as a friend, but I think being in a relationship with a man who is so damaged starts you off with a damaged relationship. It's too much.

TIMEOUT

·······························

"How Do You Make
That First Date Less Awkward?"

My first real date with Melo, I was filming with MTV on location in Long Beach, California. We met for dinner. I wore some nice jeans and a fashionable top. We went to a restaurant connected to my hotel. I brought a friend of mine who worked with me at MTV, and he brought a friend too. We both had someone to lean on if the conversation waned or got weird, so it helped to take the pressure off.

But of course we both let each other know we were bringing a friend beforehand. Don't just show up on a date with a tagalong. That's just strange. And it can be a real turnoff if it's not discussed beforehand.

There are women who like to have their girlfriends with them all the time. This is a big no-no, especially if you're to get to know a man. It's cool for the first date (provided you both discussed it), to have an icebreaker. But after that, go solo.

In the beginning of our relationship, Melo was the guy who traveled with a big entourage. At first, I wanted to be cool with all his friends. I thought that would make it better with us if his friends all liked me. But after a while it seemed as if we were never alone. I

remember thinking, "I don't know if I can do this . . ." and eventually I said, "Yo, when can it ever just be us?"

Melo is the kind of person who hates to offend people. And he's definitely not the kind of guy who will tell people to go away. But as we got closer, the entourage got smaller and smaller. I actually like most of his friends. But I liked being with just him more.

CHAPTER THREE
Personal Foul: Young and Dumb!

Personal foul: Unnecessary rough contact. It is a breach of the rules that concerns illegal personal contact with an opponent.

First love is perhaps the most fragile and most important in a woman's life. I remember being in high school wanting to experience it so badly. I would watch friends of mine fall in love and it seemed like such a fairy tale. I too wanted someone to go to Baskin-Robbins with, to the movies with, to hold hands with in the mall. I wanted to write his name and my name on the cover of my notebook inside a heart.

I didn't have that in high school. And when it finally happened for me, I wasn't ready. I did all of the wrong things. I was clueless. I wish someone had schooled me before I fell so hard. Looking back, I learned a lot from that relationship—a lot of things *not* to do, like not putting myself first, and not falling too hard too fast.

And now, I see that my sixteen-year-old cousin has her first boyfriend. I watch her posts on Instagram and I see the road she's going down. I watch and I'm tempted to warn her, but I know *how* I warn her will matter. Some of the elders in my family are dismissing the relationship, saying, "You're young. You will have dozens of boyfriends. Don't get too caught up in this one."

That's the wrong approach. While it may be true, to her this is the only guy she sees herself with forever. She's all in. And hearing our family say that it won't last will only make her work harder to prove everyone wrong. She is more likely to do something crazy with everyone telling her it's not real or he's not the one.

That's what happened with me. The more negative opinions people had, the more I shut everyone out and clung closer to him.

So I approach my cousin differently to give her some advice. I say, "I know how you feel about him and it's nice. I'm happy for you. Just remember what you do now can affect the rest of your life. You don't want to have babies yet."

I also tell her to not forget who she is.

"You're a smart and special girl," I tell her. "Value yourself. Know what you're bringing to the table. A person should be just as happy to be with you as you are to be with them. You guys look great to-

Love yourself first.

gether, but make sure you love yourself first."

That's what I would have told my eighteen-year-old self who was falling in love for the first time. I would have also told her: "Don't ever love anyone (other than God and your children) more than you love yourself."

I rode the whole eight hours from Washington, D.C., to Atlanta, crying. It was me and my dog, Blaze, all of my shit in the back of my Mazda MX-3. And my broken heart.

Somewhere around Richmond I was hoping we would hit a tree or something and I would just die. I couldn't imagine living. Not without him. But I also knew I couldn't live with him, which was why I called my father and asked him to come and get me.

This was my first love. My first true love. I was a fresh-man at Howard University. I had gotten in on an academic scholarship, but I spent most of the year doing everything but going to class.

And I didn't want to hear any negativity about my

relationship. If the people around me didn't like it, they had to go. That's what I told my mother, my father, and anyone who had an opinion about my relationship.

"If you don't accept him, then you don't accept me!" was my stance.

Looking back, I can't blame my family for not being happy with Doug (not his real name). He was much older than me, and I was clearly not focused on my education. And perhaps they saw something in him that I didn't see at the time. But I wasn't trying to see it or hear anything. Dice calls this one of the darkest periods of my life, and certainly of our deep friendship and bond, because I wasn't even really talking to her much, either. Dice was like my sister. She was closer to me than a sister and I alienated even her during this time.

My mom knew from the beginning that this man was trouble.

We both met Doug while I was making my college rounds. My mom and I had driven up the East Coast checking out schools. We went to Spelman in Atlanta, but I didn't want to be so close to home. We visited North Carolina A&T and Hampton before landing in D.C. to check out Howard. I wanted to go to a historically black college, not for the history but because back then everybody knew that's where you'd have the most fun. The HBCUs had a reputation of being party schools.

I fell in love with D.C. The city was cool, there were lots of things to do there, and they had a bunch of radio stations. I knew I wanted to be in radio, so checking out the local stations was high on my agenda. D.C. had some of the hottest radio stations in the country. Even Howard's station, WHUR, could rival any commercial station on the air anywhere.

While visiting one of D.C.'s top stations, I met one of their star deejays, Doug. He took it upon himself to show me and Mom around, telling me not only about the station but also about the city. He was cute. He had these eyes that just made you want to melt. We flirted a bit and he made me feel like I was special. I was only seventeen, and he was a grown man—with his own apartment and car—which made him even more intriguing. He wasn't like any of my high school boyfriends. (Not that I really ever had a boyfriend in high school . . . more on that later.) He just showed so much interest in me and I felt special.

I could see my mom giving me the side eye during the visit. And she would shake her head from time to time during our little tour. On the drive home she said, "If you pick this school, it won't be for the school."

"Ma, what are you talking about?!"

"I'm going to let you do what you think is best," she said and left it alone.

I did end up picking Howard. And my mother was

right—school wasn't on my list of priorities when deciding. When I got back from our tour, Doug and I talked on the phone just about every day. He seemed to be really into me. He even came to my high school graduation in Atlanta. I thought I was the shit. I had a semi-celebrity, a real man, come to my graduation. He drove all that way for me. That really sealed it. I couldn't wait to get to Howard in the fall.

When I got there, though, I spent very little time in the classroom. Most of my days were spent at the radio station hanging out with Doug, or in the clubs with him at night. Or I'd be in my dorm room waiting for him to call. Or in his apartment waiting for him to come home.

I felt like he understood me when I shared my dreams and goals, and I thought he could teach me things about the radio business I needed to know . . . among other things. His personality was very over-the-top, and very social. He was the life of the party. When he came around it was always fun times. I totally enjoyed being with him . . . at first.

My first week at Howard was a whirlwind. I couldn't wait to be with Doug and away from the watchful eye of my mother. I went with him to a club date that he was hosting. He was the man of the night and I was thrilled to be there with him as his girlfriend, watching him do his thing. I was officially in love.

Afterward we went to this hotel. I was nervous and excited and at the same time wanted to prove that I was a real woman, not a little girl. I was a virgin. It wasn't something we had discussed because I didn't want it to be a thing.

For me, being a virgin wasn't a big deal. I wasn't saving myself for marriage or anything like that. The opportunity had just never presented itself. What was crazy was that while I was very popular in high school, none of the guys I liked ever seemed to like me.

I was on the radio. I was hosting clubs. I was playing ball. I was the girl all the guys thought was cool. I was a tomboy, not one of the girls wearing the tight clothes or trying to be sexy, so I wasn't catching looks like that. And I liked being a guys' girl. I was the girl all the guys loved hanging out with, getting advice from. They respected me. I guess a little too much.

To this day, I'm still a guys' girl. I still have a lot of guy friends and I'm the one they call and ask, "Why did this chick do so and so . . . ?" I'm their buddy that they like to hang out with and get advice from. It was that way when I was a kid and it's that way today. There are advantages to being *that girl*—like you get to know what men are really thinking and you get to understand men from a whole different perspective. But there are definite disadvantages to being *that girl*, too.

I didn't even get asked to my high school senior prom. My mom told me, "Oh, somebody's going to take you!" But no one asked me. I ended up going with a random friend from another school. My mom always talks about that. She told me guys were intimidated to approach me because I was so popular and self-assured and independent. Or they just thought I already had a date.

My message to guys: Sometimes you have to take a chance with a girl you think you have no chance with, because a lot of those girls are getting zero love.

I loved being the cool popular girl, but I got tired of being seen as everyone's sister. I wanted to have a connection. I wanted to have a boyfriend. I wanted to find love. And I did when I met Doug.

I was a virgin because no one was pursuing me. Doug was one of the first guys to make me feel special in that way. I always wanted to prove I wasn't this young girl. I didn't want him to know how inexperienced I was. I tried to play it off. But I think I ended up telling him that this was my first time right before we did it and he was like, "Holy shit!"

Back then, *everybody* was having sex. I don't think any of my girlfriends were virgins. I definitely was the last of the Mohicans from my group of friends. So I was ready at this point. For him, it must have been crazy because he never suspected. But he was gentle and kind and made my first time memorable. But after he got it, I guess the thrill and excitement of being with me was over for him.

Or maybe that was just his pattern . . . on to the next.

He started coming around less and less. I started hearing rumors about other women, and our time together was spent arguing about why he wasn't spending more time with me. I used to try to cook up schemes to make him pay at-

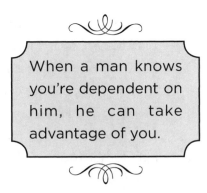

When a man knows you're dependent on him, he can take advantage of you.

tention to me. I was faking illnesses, hoping he would run to see me. I was getting really desperate, and I must have looked pretty pitiful.

Looking back, I know I opened the door for him to mistreat me because I didn't come into the relationship on my own terms. I came in as a little girl who looked up to him, and I poured my everything into him. I relied too much on him. When a man knows you're dependent on him, he can take advantage of you.

It wasn't long before I knew it was a bad decision to go to Howard for all of the wrong reasons. Once I actually arrived at Howard, things changed. Before coming to Howard, I talked to him just about every day for long periods. Even those first few months I was there were special. But things started to switch up quickly. I was no longer his priority. He stopped letting me come to the clubs where he would be hosting parties until three or four in the morning. I would wait for him, but some nights he wouldn't come home. I was technically living in the dorm at Howard. But I spent every night at Doug's.

I made the mistake of making Doug my entire center. I totally depended on him for my social life. I never made friends at school and I really didn't have a life outside of him. I made friends with his friends and his friends' girl-friends and the jocks at his radio station, who I'm still cool with today. In fact, his best friend's girlfriend at the time is still one of my best friends.

But it was a mistake for me not to have my own friends and at the same time to alienate the people who loved me. It was a big mistake, because I didn't have my own support system or shoulders to cry on when things went south. These were *his* people. Guys like Doug love it when a girl doesn't have friends and family around her. It allows them to get away with just about anything.

Doug had the car, he had the connections, he had the career. I was caught up in his life, and I never developed my own life while I was with him. This was my first year of college. I should have been immersed in being a freshman and participating in campus activities and going to school and learning. This was Howard—one of the best histori-cally black colleges in the nation. I was in the nation's capital. The Lincoln Memorial. The Washington Monu-ment. The Mall. The White House. I should have been exploring D.C., making friends, and having college fun.

Instead I was cooped up in an apartment most of the time waiting for Doug to come home.

I only went on that college tour for kicks. I really knew that I didn't need to go to college to pursue my career. I was already working at a major radio station in high school and moving up the ladder. I was learning my craft. Going to college to get a degree in communications would not give me the kind of experience I was getting every day. I knew this. So part of me was going to college to make my mom happy, but the biggest reason (which I can admit now) was because of Doug.

Don't get me wrong; despite knowing that I didn't need to go to college to pursue my career, I was still amped to go. My mom had an associate degree and I thought it would be cool to have that degree under my belt. And I was excited to go to Howard. It turned out that I didn't even get to have that college experience.

I remember the day I got accepted to Howard. We were living in LakePoint, which was this hot apartment complex across the street from Titi Edna and Dice. It was where all the cool people lived (at least that's how I saw it).

I opened the door to our apartment and there was an envelope on the doormat with the Howard symbol and gold seal. It looked so professional. I opened it and it read: "Congratulations. You have been accepted . . ." And then it talked about the scholarship package and what was included. My memory isn't always so great, but this moment is crystal clear. I can see that envelope and I remember how I felt.

I was excited, because it meant I would be going away to school and I would be on my own for the first time. It meant I was an adult. It was also an enormous accomplishment. This was Howard, one of the best schools in the country. And I got an academic scholarship.

"Somebody sent this to me!" was all I could think. I felt extremely special. I knew there was no way we could afford Howard, so getting that scholarship just made it seem to me that I was supposed to go to Howard. And Doug was in D.C.

My mom was ecstatic when she found out that I was accepted to Howard. But she started questioning my decision when Doug showed up at my high school graduation. She knew then something more was up and she didn't feel good about it.

I allowed him to rob me and my family of rejoicing in that moment. College is a great place for young people to grow and expand their knowledge base and discover themselves. But I didn't even get a chance to do that because I was so wrapped up in a man.

I also lied to myself (as we often do) and said that Doug could help me with my career. He could teach me things I didn't know about the radio business. He would help open doors for me and give me exposure in a bigger market. He didn't open a single door. I left there with a broken heart, but with even more resolve to put my life back on track, to draw up a plan for my next move.

It was crazy, because before this if you'd asked any of my friends or family if I could ever be wrapped up in a guy like this, they would have said, "Hell, no!" I was very independent. But I also had some insecurity. I can see now where I looked to him to fill in my blanks.

I didn't feel that I could turn to anyone—not even the men in my life, my dad and stepfather. As you know, John and I didn't really communicate much. He and my dad also had a pretty rocky relationship. It was so bad at one point that my stepdad had a separate line put in the house that had a special ring so that when my dad called, he wouldn't have to pick up the phone and speak to him.

The tension between my dad and my stepfather was so bad that I just didn't want to be around either one of them. I began to grow distant because the less contact I had with them, the less tension there would be. I started being more rebellious, too. I guess I was looking for a father figure (or some male authority) when I met Doug. I wanted someone I could confide in and who could teach me things. Doug was successful in an industry I wanted to be in, and I just thought everything he said was gospel. He seemed to have it all together.

A lot of girls today gravitate toward an older man who becomes a father figure to them. This is a huge mistake. No man but a father (or stepfather, or uncle) can ever fill that role in your life. It's actually kind of sick when you think of your man as being your "daddy." Emotionally, it just makes you too vulnerable and an easy target for abuse. But I totally understand the need to have that strong male figure in your life. Doug filled that role for me.

He started telling me what to do, and I thought he must know. My dad and I have a great relationship now. But he wasn't around much because of his travels and I wasn't available because once I was all in on this relationship, I shut everyone out. I turned my back on my whole family. My mom to this day, like Dice, also says this was the hardest time she went through with me. I know it hurt her deeply when she found out how he ended up treating me.

The relationship began to unravel when I began to see that the rumors weren't just rumors. He would interview celebrities and would flirt with them and I would think nothing of it initially. That was the job. Then he started having strippers come to the studio. They would come in and show off some of their moves. Then he started hosting parties in the strip clubs and I wasn't allowed to come. Then I wouldn't hear from him for a couple of days.

He had mood swings, too. We'd be eating dinner and I would ask him a question and he would fly off the handle and throw the plate of food across the room against the wall. Things like that started happening more frequently.

He bought me a Rottweiler puppy that we named

Johnny Blaze. I was a Method Man fanatic and Johnny Blaze was one of Method Man's alter egos. I loved that dog. Blaze stayed at Doug's place because I couldn't have him in the dorm, and I spent most of my time there anyway.

We were eating dinner one night and Blaze came over to the table as he always did, begging for scraps, and he put his nose close to Doug's plate. Doug got up, grabbed a broom, and whacked Blaze over the back with the stick end of the broom so hard that the stick broke.

I lost it. Blaze was my baby. It was as if Doug had beaten my child. He never put his hands on me, but that was close enough. I put up with the cheating, the humiliation, the rage, and the embarrassment. But hitting Blaze like that woke something up inside me. I was done.

I was crying hysterically, and when he left I called my father and asked him to come get me. My dad didn't ask any questions. He flew in, packed up my things and my dog, and we hit the road back home to Atlanta.

On that drive back, I thought of all the times when I should have left but didn't.

One time, he was making an appearance at a club, and he was in the deejay booth, on the microphone. I was near the booth in the crowd, watching him, as proud as I could be. A woman walked up to me and said, "I need to talk to you!"

"About what?" I said. I didn't know her.

She lifted up her shirt and said, "I'm pregnant!"

"So? Why are you telling me this?"

"Your man's the father!"

At this point Doug must have seen what was happening, and he made his way over to us.

"You're lying!" I said, and we had an epic argument that shut the club down. It was crazy, because I never got into arguments—especially not over a man. It's not my style. But Doug was right there alongside me, calling her a liar, so I felt I had a right.

About a month later, he sat me down and told me that this woman was indeed having his baby. He said he had taken a paternity test, which I later found out was a lie. He knew all along that the baby was his. He said he wanted me to come with him to the hospital to see the baby; it was a girl.

I was devastated. People, his friends, had been telling me that he was wild, and there were more than enough women willing to tell me that they were sleeping with him. But I brushed it all off because (a) I didn't want to believe it, (b) he was a celebrity in town, and of course, people wanted to claim they were with him, and (c) I was just stupid.

After months of not speaking to my mom the way I used to, I picked up the phone and called her and told her what had happened.

"Now you're going to the hospital to see his baby? You've got to get your mind right!" she told me.

I told him I didn't want to go to the hospital with him. But I still didn't want to be without him, either. I wanted to ride or die with him. I didn't want him to think I was jumping ship. And he was good at sweet-talking me and making me believe that he was sorry. He ended up not spending any time with his daughter, and I was happy about that. I felt like we could pretend that it never happened.

Back then, I was clueless. I didn't know to judge a man based on how he treated his kids. Instead of thinking, "What kind of man would abandon his kid?" I was thinking, "Great, he's going to be spending more time with me."

How dumb! Not only was he not spending time with his kid, but he still wasn't spending time with me. I heard he was messing around with another girl—a cheerleader for the Washington Redskins. That really hit my self-esteem. I was still a bit of a tomboy, and we all know how a cheerleader looks. I couldn't compete with that, I thought.

It was just piling up. So when he hit Blaze with that broomstick, it all hit me, too. It was time to go. When I left, I didn't hear from him for a couple of days. He must have figured I'd be back. I always came back. I had left before, going back to my dorm for a day or two. I always came back. He didn't take it seriously.

I didn't take his calls. I was able to move back into my old life in Atlanta, which I needed to do to get my mind off Doug.

I had plenty of time to think after leaving. I came to

the conclusion that my relationship with Doug was completely unhealthy. *You think?* That relationship made me never want to give of myself that way to any man again. I have to admit that I have held back just a little of myself in every relationship since. I never wanted anyone to have my whole heart to just crush it in his hands like that ever again. It was just too painful.

I let this man ruin what should have been a wonderful college experience.

I know people who say they remember going to Howard with me. But those months I spent there were a complete blur. I don't remember anything beyond being with Doug. I have no recollection, which is sad.

> No matter how bad you feel, no matter how horrible a situation seems, even if you think this person is the love of your life and you can't go on without him . . . you can! There will always be another relationship. You will survive it. You just will.

When I'm having a bad time of it, Dice will reference that period of my life to remind me that it's never *that* bad. She'll say, "If you got over [Doug] you can get over anything."

It was the worst anyone in my family had seen me, except when I lost my grandmother. This period with Doug was damn near unbearable. I didn't want to eat. I couldn't sleep. I didn't want to live.

But what I also learned was that no matter how bad you feel, no matter how horrible a situation seems, even if you think this person is the love of your life and you can't go on without him . . . you can! There will always be another relationship. You will survive it. You just will.

The other valuable lesson I learned was that when you're ready to go, just leave. There is something better around the corner. It may not be that next dude, but it may be something even better. For me, had I not left when I did, I probably would not have ended up in Los Angeles on a top-rated radio show, which eventually led me back home to New York as a member of one of the hottest shows on television at the time—*TRL*.

CHAPTER FOUR

The Playbook:
Have a Game Plan

Playbook: 1. A book containing a range of possible set plays. 2. A notional range of possible tactics in any sphere of activity.

One of the best things I learned from being in that relationship with Doug was that you should never tie your future to a man. I'm not saying that being in a relationship or having love in your life shouldn't be part of your future. The right man will want you to be your best and pursue your dreams. A man who truly loves you will support you. Doug totally took me off my course. But because I had a game plan, I was able to get back on track.

I'd known I wanted to work in radio since I was a

teenager. Not everyone knows what they want to do with their life at such an early age, but I believe that everyone should have some idea of what they want to do and be before they get into a relationship. If you go into a serious relationship and you don't have a clue about what you'd like to do, then your future becomes all about him and his dreams. And while it's great to support your man through his dreams, you won't be happy unless you have some dreams and goals of your own, too.

My dream was to be a radio personality.

When I got back to Atlanta, I went to my former radio station, WHTA, and got my old job back. I called and told them, "College didn't work out. I realized how valuable the hands-on training I got working with you guys was . . ." They welcomed me back with open arms.

And I was happy to be back.

I was able to go back so easily because of how I left. My mom always told me, "It's not your entrance, but your exit." How you leave a place is just as important as how you arrive. A lot of times people, especially young people, quit a job and they go out blazing with both middle fingers in the air. But you never know when you may need that place and those people again.

When I left WHTA they didn't replace me. That made it even easier to go back and settle into my old position. I knew my role. I wasn't one of the stars; I was an accessory to the show. I wasn't part of the credits or the drops, which said, "You're checking out Chris Lova and Poon Daddy." There was never any mention of me in the promos. It was all about them. And I was fine with that. I was happy to be in the background, on the air and making money doing it.

I had started working at WHTA in high school. During the summer heading into my junior year, I was hanging out in downtown Atlanta at the opening of the Wu-Tang store. Remember, I was a Method Man fanatic. There were these kids there handing out flyers and putting up posters for some event that WHTA was hosting. I asked one of them why they were doing that. They told me they were interning at the radio station and started telling me all the exciting things they were doing there. I knew I wanted to be down.

I called the station the next day and told them I wanted to apply to be an intern. The receptionist told me that I had to send in a résumé and I had to be eighteen. I typed up a résumé that embellished my experience and of course, my age. I had just turned sixteen that June. The station called me in for an interview with the program director. After about an hour of me talking, he hired me on the spot.

I was really into music and was able to talk about every hot rapper or artist, new or old. I was the girl who knew every word to "Represent" off of Nas's *Illmatic* album. I knew every single song ever done by Method Man. I instantly clicked at WHTA. After a couple of weeks, I was doing everything.

I caught the eye of Chaka Zulu, the music director there. In many ways he was even more important than the program director, who was more of an administrator and facilitator. Chaka Zulu was the man. He was the one who decided what actually got on the air. New artists were wooing him constantly.

I loved being in his office because he had wall-to-wall CDs and tapes. I was in heaven. He really took my music game to a whole other level, and I ended up becoming his personal intern. It just happened. I spent so much time running errands and doing odd jobs for him that people just started referring to me as Chaka's intern. I did everything that was asked of me, big or small tasks, and did it the best I could. It's important to be reliable and effective; opportunities come to those who work hard!

Chaka started giving me more and more responsibilities. He asked me to work the night shift with one of the hottest teams on the station—Chris Lova Lova and Poon Daddy. During the commercial breaks, I would get into it with Chris and Poon about some artist or song. Before I knew it, they were opening a microphone for me and we were having these discussions on the air. This was very unusual at the time. Very few women were doing radio on a rap show. You had women on R&B stations and a few hip-hop, of course. But hard-core rap was a male-dominated domain. I soon became a regular.

I was sixteen, working from ten to two in the morning, three to four days a week. And I couldn't have been happier. My mom was really cool about it, too. She knew how much I loved what I was doing, so she made a deal with me. I could do the show as long as I kept my grades up. I was a straight-A student at the time. School came pretty easy for me, so this job didn't get in the way at all.

I was independent and worked hard to be so, always. I had a beat-up blue Jetta that I saved up to buy. Ever since moving to Atlanta as a teenager, I always had a job. I worked after school at Baskin-Robbins. And on the weekends I had a job as a receptionist for a tattoo parlor before getting a job at the radio station. I would drive to the station. On some nights I would bring my cousin Dice with me to keep me company. The station was in a not-so-nice neighborhood, and having her there made it a little less scary. I remember us having so much fun. Dice would answer the phones. She would take caller information for the winners of the contests or giveaways we would run. Back then, we used CDs, and Dice would line up the CDs in the order that we were going to play them and have them ready for us to be on the air. I loved when she was there with me.

After I left the studio, I would catch maybe four or five hours of sleep and be up and out for school. I'd do a nap after school most afternoons before going to the studio to work. I did that until I graduated and moved to D.C.

> You can never be totally lost as long as you have a game plan.

I thought moving to D.C. was the right play for my game. We do that sometimes—convince ourselves that we're making a good move, when really we're just giving up our power and following behind someone else. If I had just stayed focused . . . I knew what I wanted to do, which at my age was half the battle. I had it all figured out—everything but myself.

My playbook took a major hit in D.C. But I learned that just because you made a couple of wrong moves didn't mean that you couldn't fix it. Sometimes we also get so discouraged or mad at ourselves that we don't do the work to get back in the game.

Once I left D.C., I got back on my plan. That was one of the things that made it easier getting over Doug, too. I had something else to focus on—my career. Sometimes you will lose focus on your journey and get off plan. But if you have a plan, it's a whole lot easier to get back to it. You can never be totally lost as long as you have a game plan.

When I came back to Atlanta, I even moved out on my

own. After being away at college, it was hard for me to move back in with my mom and brother. I was used to my independence—not that my mom had a whole lot of strings attached to me. I just felt like it was time for me to be an adult.

Chris Lova Lova had a rapping partner named 4-Ize. He was always around the studio and he and I became good friends. He told me he was looking for a roommate and I was looking for a place, so we decided to move in together. You could see from a mile away that there was nothing going on between 4-Ize and me. It was strictly platonic. Of course, I could have lived with a girlfriend, but he asked first. Neither one of us could afford our own place, so it was the perfect arrangement. I bought a waterbed for my room. And we had no furniture in the living room—not even a couch. But I was on my own.

During this time Chris was rapping on the side, producing his own music. He was meeting with labels and nobody was biting. He had a song that he put out independently called "Phat Rabbit" that started to pick up steam locally. Then one day he comes in and announces, "I'm leaving the radio station!"

He told us that he was going to load up his car with his CDs and drive around the country selling them from his car.

"I'm going to see what happens," he said.

THE Love PLAYBOOK

I thought it was incredibly brave of him. Nobody was trying to sign him, but Chris believed in himself enough to put it all on the line. Do or die. He headed out on the road as Ludacris and the rest is history.

Chris gave a month's notice. While I was happy for him, I knew that after he left, the show would probably not last long. He was so dynamic on the air and he was the driving force behind its success. If I wanted to take my radio career to the next level, I knew I had to do what Chris was doing and venture out on my own.

I got this industry book that listed the top radio stations in the country. I got the addresses and names for the program directors and sent my aircheck to ten markets, which included Los Angeles, Chicago, Philly, and D.C.

About a week later, I got calls from Chicago, Philly, and even D.C., but it was the phone call from the station in L.A. that caught my attention. They said they were hiring some new people and they would like to bring me out to L.A. I had never traveled that far in my life. I was still a teenager. They asked me what my current salary was. At the time, I was making something like $15,000 a year. But I told them I was making $30,000, just throwing a number out there. They said, "We can double your salary."

What?! Double my salary!

They hired me over the phone. I was going to replace Big Lez on the midday (10 a.m.–1 p.m.) show. My mom and I flew out to Los Angeles that week on a buddy pass from my dad. They put us up in corporate housing for thirty days. My mom stayed with me for a while to get me settled. Keep in mind I was only nineteen, I had just gone through the heartbreak of my life, and I was now in Los Angeles about to make more money than I could ever have imagined, doing what I loved.

I went from feeling like my life was over to living my dream. After I'd been there just a short time they gave me the 6 p.m.–10 p.m. spot. I was loud and boisterous and they felt that would play well with the young after-school and college-age crowd. And it did. I was on my way to radio stardom—and then my phone rang out of the blue.

It was Doug.

He'd heard I was doing well in Los Angeles and he had lost his job. He wanted to come out to L.A. to see if there was anything out there for him. He asked if he could hang with me while he got settled.

Of course, I said. Yes . . . I know. I know. What was I thinking? I swear, as soon as you're getting over someone and doing well, they always seem to creep back in. I wish I had said no and kept it moving. But I was lonely. I didn't know anyone in L.A. My mom had gone back to Atlanta. And though I was doing well on my own, I missed him. That's the thing about that crazy love—it can suck you back in at a moment's notice. He came with his apologies and sweet talk and I was a sucker for it all.

I guess I was still hoping that maybe we could make it

work. And now that he was in my territory, I'd be in control. I was the one who was established. I had been in L.A. for about a year at this point, and I felt like now I would have the upper hand.

He'd been staying with me for about a month and we had rekindled our relationship a little, when I got a call from some girl. She said she was pregnant with Doug's baby. "And he up and left me!" *Déjà vu!* She sent me a picture of the sonogram to prove it.

I confronted him and he said, "She's lying!"

"It's always 'She's lying'!" I said. "Get out!"

He refused to leave. Before this, when I would hear about friends trying to kick someone out and they refused to go, I would think that was ridiculous. I mean, how could someone refuse to leave when they're told to? Well, I totally understood it now. Because he sat in my living room, arms crossed, and he wasn't budging.

I finally had to call a couple of male friends of mine to help.

"I'm in a bad situation," I told them. "He is refusing to leave and I need him to go."

About ten minutes later, three of my very large and intimidating friends showed up. Doug was mad as hell, but after they arrived he understood what would happen if he didn't leave. He got his stuff, and they drove him to the airport and put his ass on the next thing smoking back to D.C.

Rich Nice, a producer that I'm still cool with, was one of my buddies who came to my rescue that day. I'll never forget that they did that. They saved me. I have no idea what I was thinking, letting Doug back in, but I can say it's real easy to fall back into a rut with someone that you know isn't good for you.

Sometimes you think being with that dude is better than being alone. I'm here to tell you, it's not! It's far better to be alone.

The other lesson I've learned the hard way is that you should wait to give that person your heart until he shows you his true self. When you first meet, you aren't meeting who he really is. But had I waited and watched, I would have seen who Doug really was. I would have seen that he was just a player. Instead, I thought I was special and he was saying those sweet things only to me and nobody else.

I moved on quickly after he left, and got back to my life and working hard. I spent the next year and a half in L.A. enjoying being single and learning to live with myself and for myself.

Great things were happening for me professionally, but I didn't have a man. Somehow it made the experience less important to me. Isn't that crazy? How many women are out there doing fantastic things but aren't enjoying them because they're miserable because they don't have a man?

That was me. I was doing all of these great things in my career, but I didn't have anyone to share it with. At that time in my life, I felt that if I didn't have a man, I didn't have value. I guess it goes back to my need for attention.

I wasn't completely alone in L.A. After I got settled, I sent for Blaze, who was staying with a friend of mine in Atlanta. They put his big ass on a plane and sent him out to me, and I was so happy. After work and before I had a club date, I'd take Blaze to the dog park. Having him with me made me less lonely.

It's so important that you have a life, especially after a breakup. If you don't have one, you'd better find one or create one. That should be in your playbook. And even in a relationship when things are going well, you still have to have your own life. Your life can't be his life and it can't be all about him. Your life also can't be all about you. If you want a man in your life, you have to carve out space for him to fit in. Women who pour themselves totally into their careers miss out, too.

For me, I left room for my dog, for my friends, and for fun. I was done with men for a while. I also recommend that when you've gone through a rough relationship patch, you take some time to reboot your life. Get back in touch with yourself and clear your head. Take the time to remember who you are and what's most important to you.

If you jump right into another relationship, you will definitely be bringing some of the crap with you from your previous relationship. And while that rebound relationship may be a fun distraction in the beginning, it can totally end in more heartache and pain. (Now, rebound sex is fine . . . just not a rebound relationship.)

Learn to be by yourself for a minute. I guarantee you will learn some things about what went wrong and prevent it from ever happening again.

After the breakup with Doug in D.C., I decided to be bold. I took that job in Los Angeles, which felt like a complete free fall without a net. I was scared, but I did it because I had nothing to lose. I was miserable in my personal life; I had failed at love. I needed to pursue something and see if I could make it work for myself.

TIMEOUT

....

How Can I Change a Player?

"I really like this guy that I met, but he's a player. He's a ladies' man. Is it possible to change him into a one-woman man?"

And as my Mami Nina always said, you can't change someone. You don't enter a relationship ready to change, and you can't expect your partner to change once you start dating. Of course, people grow and evolve while they're in relationships, hopefully in har-

What you see is what you get with a man.

mony. But you shouldn't get serious with a guy if you're expecting to change the very core of who he is and how he acts.

For the most part, what you see is what you get with a man. They may play games or try to muster up some swagger when you're first dating. But their true colors always come through.

But . . . there are times when a man is motivated to change. He *wants* to change in order to have what

he wants. That's different than trying to change someone. Sometimes you have to present the right motivation for him to want to change. I have seen several cases where that's exactly what happened.

My mom's brother was a cop. Growing up in Brooklyn, he had a lot of girls. He was cute, and he had a lot of style. Nobody thought he would ever settle down. But then he met "the one." When he found that woman, she brought something to the table that made him want to commit and settle down. He wanted to be with her. And in order for that to happen, he had to change—give up the other girls and get serious.

Today, he and my aunt Pauline have been together more than twenty years, and they are happy and he is devoted to her. So can a woman change a ladies' man? Yes. By being the kind of motivation that will make him want to change. She has to bring to the table all the things that will make him forget about everyone else.

CHAPTER FIVE
One-on-One: Friendship First!

One-on-one: 1. Playing directly against a single opposing player. 2. Involving a direct encounter between one person and another.

I believe the best way to find Mr. Right, so to speak, is to find a friend first. When I watch successful relationships, what I see most often is couples who genuinely like each other. They're friends. I believe in love and butterflies and flowers and candy and all that. But that comes in waves in a relationship. When that new love with the butterflies wears off, what's left? If the relationship started off as a friendship, you still have someone you like hanging out with, eating dinner with, going to the movies with, sharing your life with.

A solid marriage starts with a solid friendship. If it's all about the physical attraction, how do you keep it going when that wanes? What do you have to talk about? Being married to your friend should feel like a sleepover every night (maybe not every single night, but you get what I'm saying). If you're not friends and problems creep in (because they always do), your relationship will not be able to stand up to the trials and tests.

Most of my relationships started as friends. I believe that's the best recipe for success. If you're friends first, you already have broken down so many of the barriers and the fronts that people put up in relationships. He's seen you without makeup, looking like a bum, and you've been around him when he's farting and in a bad mood. He's seen you and been there for you when you've had trouble on your job. You were there when he had a fight with someone in his family, and you talked him through it. He was there when you were sick as a dog with the flu and brought you soup. You were there for him when he was lonely and just wanted someone to play video games with and talk to.

When you're friends, after seeing each other at your worst, y'all still like each other. So if and when that spark hits—you know, that spark that makes the bottom of your stomach jump when he's around—it's just natural to take things to the next level.

And when those tingly feelings and butterflies and all

of the lust that comes with new love wear off—because they eventually always do—you still have your buddy. And it's a lot easier to reignite those embers when you really *like* the one you're with.

Carmelo and I started as friends . . .

A couple of years into my radio stint in Los Angeles, I got a call from New York. They said they wanted me to be a host of MTV's *Direct Effect* with DJ Clue. It was a hip-hop show and I was making a name for myself as a hip-hop chick.

I had been working on the show for about six months when they approached me about hosting *Total Request Live*. What? That was huge! Carson Daly was leaving and they were testing out different hosts. To say this was a much bigger platform is an understatement. On *Direct Effect*, it was a certain kind of flow and I was interviewing rappers. *TRL* was mainstream. I couldn't get on *TRL* talking about "Yo, yo, son . . . !" *TRL* La La had to be different from *Direct Effect* La La, and I knew I could pull it off. My immersion in world news as a kid came in handy . . . thanks to my stepdad.

TRL was a game changer. It not only exposed me to a broader audience, but I also knew that there'd never been an African-American Hispanic in the studio every day on a show like that. MTV had Sway. But he did the news. And there was Ananda Lewis. But she was more "exotic." She didn't necessarily come off as black. I was very proud to represent.

TRL was the hottest show on television at the time for a young demographic, and everybody in the industry, not just music folks, wanted to appear on it. It taped live in the middle of Times Square. The studio had floor-to-ceiling windows and you could look out and see that giant Nissin Cup o' Noodles where they dropped the ball every New Year. And you could look down on the screaming crowd of teenagers that packed Times Square when we were on. It was surreal. These kids would come there just for a glimpse of whoever would be on set that day. You could see anyone from John Travolta to Madonna, Mariah Carey to Denzel Washington. It was bananas and I was going to be a part of it. I was twenty-one years old, making six figures, and on the hottest show in the world.

I was pulling double duty on MTV. After *TRL*, I would still go and host *Direct Effect*. I would go from interviewing Tom Cruise in one hour on *TRL* to chilling with Mobb Deep the next.

Clue and I, of course, became very close. We were on the air together every day. I would host club dates with him at least twice a week. I was loving this crazy, fast-paced New York life. I was settling back into the town of my youth. I had a fly apartment in trendy Edge-water, New Jersey. I had a brand-new Mercedes-Benz truck, and I was open to having a relationship. I would always complain to Clue about being in New York and not having that special someone to hang out with. It was high school all over again. Guys weren't approaching me, and if they were it was for me to help them with their career. "Can you introduce me to [fill in the blank]" was what I was hearing.

I said to Clue, "Hook me up with somebody good." And he would say, "You don't want me to hook you up . . ."

This one time I asked him, it was the exact moment that he was getting a text from his boy Carmelo Anthony. He looked at his phone and looked at me and said, "Oh, shit . . . I think I have somebody for you to meet."

"Who?"

"Carmelo Anthony."

I knew the name. He had been a college phenom and had won the NCAA championship for Syracuse. He was in Denver. Denver wasn't on my map at all. And I wasn't a big college basketball fan, so I really didn't know much about him outside of his championship at Syracuse.

"He's an NBA basketball player," Clue told me. "He just got drafted."

"A basketball player? And a rookie?! For real? You must think I have 'stupid' written across my forehead!"

I just wasn't interested. A rookie to me was someone young and inexperienced in life. And a rookie baller? He had to be just out there running crazy, burning through those millions and all of the female opportunities.

Clue kind of laughed. "No," he said, reassuring me. "He's mad cool. I wouldn't do you like that."

"Nah, that's okay."

"It's not the end of the world. Just hang out and see how it goes."

Melo was in town and he just happened to be at the club where Clue was hosting that night. I remember seeing this very tall, handsome man surrounded by a bunch of girls, and I knew it was Carmelo Anthony. I went over and introduced myself and told him Clue told me he was cool. He said he knew who I was. And we chatted very briefly. I kept it casual and kept it moving. I'm sure I was thinking, "This is not going anywhere."

I was hanging in the VIP section with Clue and a few of my friends, and Carmelo sent a bottle over to our table.

"This is so predictable," I thought, but I drank the champagne and thanked him from across the room, holding a glass up. Drinks on him! When he was ready to leave, he came over to our section.

"What are you doing after this?" he said.

After this? It was three o'clock in the morning. I told him I was going home and going to sleep. I had to work the next day.

"Okay, get home safe. I'm here in New York for a minute. Maybe we can hang out."

"I'll see what Clue's doing tomorrow and I'll get up with y'all."

"Why does Clue have to be around for us to hang out?" he asked.

That stuck out for me and I tucked it away for future consideration. That was the first sign that he liked me. He wanted to see me alone. For some reason, however, we could never seem to catch up with each other during his stay in New York. We would make plans and we kept canceling on each other. But we talked a lot on the phone. This is where our friendship really blossomed. The conversation never got romantic, but we had a lot in common and of course, my love of basketball had us debating stuff like who is the best player of all time all night long.

That summer, I was in Long Beach, California. Every summer back then, MTV would move to the MTV Beach House, where the entire MTV team would move into a house together in some hot city—from Miami to Lake Tahoe. That summer it was Long Beach. Those were some of the most memorable times of my life. When you're living it, you're not thinking about it. But looking back, I know there will never be another time like that. To be young, free, in the mix, and having a blast . . . priceless.

One afternoon I got a phone call.

"Where are you?" It was Melo.

I told him I was in Long Beach.

He said, "I'm thinking about making a pit stop. I'll come through and check you out."

It wasn't like he was coming just to see me. (Or so I thought at the time.) I knew Nelly was shooting a video near there and he and Nelly were friends. I was like, "Cool, let me know."

"I'm getting on a plane now and I'll be there."

After I hung up, I got butterflies thinking about seeing him. *Uh-oh.* I was getting a little nervous because I was starting to like him. And I knew he was starting to like me, too. He would say little things that let me know he liked me.

A couple of hours later, I got another call from him.

"Yo, bad weather. The flight couldn't take off. I'm not coming."

I was so disappointed.

Then he started laughing. "I'm just kidding! I'm at the hotel across the way."

We laughed and that was a moment for me when I knew: "I really like this guy."

That night we went out to eat. The next day he said he was driving to Los Angeles to hang out with Nelly on the set of his video. *Oh, brother.* I thought Melo was going to get on that video set and I wouldn't hear from him. Back then, video sets for rappers were notorious playgrounds. What young man wouldn't get sucked into all of that? But

Melo said he was coming back to hang out and he did. He was back in time for us to go to dinner. He didn't owe me that. We hung out alone that night instead of with his entourage and mine. And that's when we had our first kiss.

That weekend there was a major boxing match in Vegas. Melo said he was going and invited me and some of my friends to hang out with him in Vegas. I and a couple of my girlfriends who were chilling with me in Long Beach rented a car and drove to Vegas. It was the best road trip ever. We shared a room in Vegas, and after checking in, we went to Melo's room—or should I say his suite? It was huge. I wasn't used to walking into the biggest hotel rooms in Vegas. It was incredible. We three girls were crashing in one room together, and here he had this whole floor in a major casino. It was crazy.

It was the night of the fight. My friends had scattered and so did his. It was Vegas. Nobody wanted to sit in a room in Vegas all night. There's just too much to do there. It was time for the fight and I didn't have tickets. Melo had gotten his ticket through his sports connection a while back and the fight was sold out.

"You know, I don't really want to go," he said.

"What?!"

"I'm not going," he said.

"But you came here just to go to the fight!" I said.

He didn't go and it was great. We spent the night talking. We ordered room service and had a great time. As the night went on, I was itching to gamble. Everyone knows I love to gamble. Back then I was playing the $5 and $10 blackjack tables. As we headed into the casino, we were stopped by security.

"We need to see your ID," they said.

You have to be twenty-one to go into the casinos. That's when I found out that Carmelo wasn't of age. *You have got to be kidding me!* I was shocked. He was nineteen when we met. I assumed he was older. I don't know why. I just did. He was in the club, sending over bottles—of course he was over twenty-one.

Had I known he was only nineteen when we met, I never would have given him the time of day. He would not have stood a chance. I felt crazy enough when I found out his age, but it was too late then. When I told my friends, they started teasing me about robbing the cradle and calling me Mrs. Robinson. I was only a few years older than he was, but he was so young that it mattered. We definitely wouldn't have gotten to the point where I could fall in love had I known his age. I guess it was fate that I didn't.

I was only twenty-two myself, but girls typically mature faster than guys. I had been grown (in my mind) a long time. Come to find out, he wasn't a typical nineteen-year-old. While there were areas where he was definitely young (because as an elite baller he was coddled and taken care of from an early age), he also had responsibilities that many men his age simply never did. He was a multimillionaire. He had a full-time job that required that he perform at a high level and have a strong work ethic. He owned his own home, a large property in Denver. He had cars. He had a chef. He was a man.

I tried to stop thinking about his age, and to judge him on how he acted.

After Vegas, I was shocked twice. Because in addition to discovering his age, I also discovered that I was falling in love.

When we first met, there were a few sparks, but I quickly put them out. I was adamant about not dating a professional basketball player. I was cautious because of the stereotypes. So I kept my feelings at bay. I really had to think about whether I wanted to enter that kind of world. Initially, I decided that I didn't.

But about three or four months into the friendship, it was becoming something and I couldn't deny it anymore. When we were apart, he was saying that he missed me and that his life felt emptier without me—things buddies didn't say to each other.

A few months after Vegas, during basketball season, Melo asked me to come visit him in Denver. He was in the throes of his first NBA season and couldn't come to see me in New York. I remember one night we were on the phone and he was saying that he needed me there.

"I have a job. I have to work. I can't just pick up and leave," I told him.

"What time do you have to be there?" he asked me.

I told him.

"Okay. I'll have a plane waiting for you when you get off. You can come see me and be back in New York in time for your show tomorrow."

I had a car pick me up from my apartment and take me to Teterboro Airport in New Jersey. I had never flown private before and it was all very exciting. I never let on, though. I played it real cool, like I flew private all the time.

I got to the airport, gave them the plane number. Someone came and got my bags and escorted me to the tarmac and onto the plane. No security checks. No drama. I was the only one on the plane. Just me and the pilot. I was taking pictures and sending them to my friends. The plane was like some fancy conference room with its plush seating. This was the life.

I made that trip several times, and each time I was getting pulled in. Each trip brought me closer and closer. Before I knew it, I was in love. I couldn't wait to see him again. And he was asking me to come every week and then every other day. I clearly remember days of flying to Denver for a few days, landing in New York and going straight to MTV to tape *TRL* and getting off work and flying right back to Denver. I'd be dead tired, but I never let anyone know that I literally had just gotten off the plane and gone straight on the air.

I knew he was in love, too. Guys aren't the most communicative beings, so when they start saying things like "I miss you!" and "Life's not the same without you," you start getting clues that they're falling for you. That and not being able to get enough of you.

We were together all the time. We were having fun, enjoying one another, just the two of us.

Then I got pregnant.

TIMEOUT

And Baby Makes Three . . . but What About the Two?

Becoming a mother affected our relationship. Your whole world changes in an instant. It's no longer about you and your husband; it's now all about the child. But if you want to keep your relationship healthy, you're going to have to balance the baby time with the couple time. Your kids will be happier in the long run if you have a healthy, happy marriage.

I know a couple whose entire lives revolve around their kid. Their child does everything with them . . . literally. They don't go anywhere without their kid. They won't even let anyone babysit for them.

My question is, "When do you guys have time for each other?"

You need to spend time away from your kid and focus on just the two of you every now and then. You should go on vacations without the kid and definitely have date nights where it's all about you and him. I'm so involved that I want Kiyan around all the time. But I know that Melo and I need our time, too, to have adult time. I used to feel bad when I didn't

include Kiyan in everything we did. But there are things he doesn't need to be exposed to.

With children, you want to be a great parent, but you can't forget to nurture your relationship because I believe that's part of good parenting.

I've heard people say a thousand times, "We stayed together for the kids." I've seen people in miserable relationships who damn near hate each other, but they stayed together twenty years. For the kids?

That's classic. And while some people applaud that, I don't. I think if you're staying together just for the kids and you're miserable, your kids know it, and it creates a whole different kind of dysfunction. What child feels good while Mommy or Daddy or both are miserable, having secret fights or just not speaking to each other day to day, but they're "staying together" for his or her sake?

Kids know. Kids are smart. And while you may think you're hiding something, you're not. You end up doing more damage. So don't use your children as an excuse for staying in a bad relationship.

And if you want to keep your relationship going well, be sure to make time for each other and make the relationship as much about the two of you as about your kids.

CHAPTER SIX

The Scrimmage:
Pros and Cons of Shacking Up

Scrimmage: *An unofficial game between two teams in a practice situation.*

Let me back up to . . . before I got pregnant.

It was Christmas Day 2003, and Melo and I were going through all the gifts under the tree in Denver. I love Christmas—it's my favorite holiday—and there were so many presents under the tree that year, I didn't know where to begin. I was like a real kid.

But there was nothing over-the-top among the gifts. I got to the last box and there were some pajamas in it. I thought, "That's cool . . . but is that it?"

At the end of the night, after dinner, he just said out of the blue, "I want to spend the rest of my life with you. Do you want to spend the rest of your life with me?" and he handed me a box.

I said yes!

This wasn't a one-knee proposal. He didn't call my parents and ask for permission. It wasn't traditional. But it was romantic and I was ecstatic. I had no idea it would take six years from that Christmas Day proposal to finally tie the knot.

Six years!

I began to wonder if we would ever get married. I wasn't the only one thinking it. The media had jokes calling me the "eternal fiancée." I thought that maybe I had made a mistake by moving in with him.

What was his incentive to get married? We were engaged, living together; we now had a child. He was getting all the benefits without having to actually say "I do."

I know you've heard the saying "Why buy the cow when you can get the milk for free?" It's something my mother used to say to me all the time. Melo was getting the milk, the cheese, the cream, everything.

I've had a few friends over the years who found themselves in a similar situation, and my advice to them was "Don't live with him! Don't play house."

Now here I was, *not* taking my own advice.

The good news was that Melo really did love me and I

believed that he wanted to marry me; he just didn't have a compelling enough reason to actually go through with it. I believe it's that way with most men. I don't know too many men who are begging to get married, who are just jumping for joy and running to the altar. For most men, marriage is a necessary evil that they agree to because they love a woman and they want her to be happy or because it's what you're supposed to do. But if they can have everything without that piece of paper, they're thinking, "What difference does it make?"

What really changed it for me was having Kiyan. It wasn't just having our son; it was also what we went through to have him. It could have either made us or broken us. But his birth brought us even closer together.

People keep asking me when I'm going to have another kid, and I always say that we're happy with the dynamic of our family. The truth is, I had the worst pregnancy of all time and I'm just not interested in going through what I went through ever again.

I had a condition called hyperemesis gravidarum. I had never heard of it before they diagnosed me with it. Apparently, less than one percent of women ever get it. It is perpetual morning sickness. Actually, it's morning-noon-and-night sickness. It's throwing up and being nauseous practically 24/7 for your entire pregnancy.

You really get to test your relationship when you're going through something like that. You really get to see how much he loves you. Most guys don't handle sickness well—not their own or anyone else's. But Melo was really cool about it. I know he felt bad. But he tried to keep my spirits up and make me as comfortable as possible—even when it got unbearable.

It got so bad that I had to have an IV line in my house during my eighth and ninth months. I would carry a barf bag everywhere with me just in case. I couldn't hold anything down—not even water. The doctors told me if I could hold down the food for even three minutes that would be good because at least some nutrients from the food could be absorbed into my body. But that wasn't happening, hence the IV.

To say I was miserable is an understatement. My misery was compounded by being in Denver—actually, not even Denver, but a secluded suburb in the boondocks near Denver. I was in this huge house alone most of the time because I was pregnant during the biggest stretch of the NBA season and Melo was either on the road or practicing.

I was seven months pregnant and still trying to work every day on *TRL*. But because of the sickness, I finally had to stop working. I went from New York to Denver, which is totally not like New York. Great people, just not a lot to do.

I was sick all the time, away from the hustle of the city, and I just felt as if I was missing out on so much. That year All-Star Weekend was in Las Vegas. And I couldn't travel.

I was miserable. It was the first time All-Star Weekend had been in Vegas, and everybody was there, calling and checking in on me, but I couldn't be there. I had just jumped into this basketball world and it was still very fresh and exciting. I felt like everybody was having fun and I was stuck.

I was a wreck. I was crying my eyes out every day. I hardly gained weight during the pregnancy. It just all felt very wrong. I used to fantasize about getting pregnant and having a baby and how beautiful it would all be. I had heard some amazing stories from friends about their experiences. Mine was so strange, and I had no one to talk with who could understand what I was going through.

I went on the Internet looking for other women going through the same thing, and I found these chat rooms and message boards for women suffering from hyperemesis gravidarum. I finally felt like I wasn't totally alone. It felt good to connect with other women who knew what I was talking about. No one had any solutions, but it just felt good to know that I wasn't alone.

My mom always laughs when we talk about my "condition."

"What are the chances?" she said. "We can't get those kinds of odds for the Lotto, but we can get something like this?"

We decided to induce labor to make sure Melo would be there for the birth. I didn't want him to be somewhere across the country. We picked March 7, because the Nuggets had a couple of days off, followed by a couple of home games. That day couldn't come quick enough for me.

The night before, we checked in and started the inducing process. By the next morning, the doctor said that my contractions had started and I was relieved. It was finally happening.

Melo said he was going to get something to eat. He had been there the entire night and through the day. He was gone for so long, I began to wonder exactly where he went to eat, the next state? Then the doctor came in and said, "It looks like we're ready to go."

What? After planning this out for months to make sure Melo would be here, he might actually miss the birth!

I called him and found out that he'd gone back home.

"Babe, they said it would take a while and I wanted to take a shower," he told me.

I was fuming. But the doctor was able to hold up the process until he got back. He was there all those hours, and the one time he stepped out, look what happened.

Kiyan was only five pounds and nine ounces. I had pre-term labor. They had to give me steroid shots for his lungs. But he was here. Having a child made this relationship real. We were a family, and now we had to be *officially* a family on paper.

Melo and I had discussed having children before we had Kiyan and we'd talked about how we wanted to raise those children. Melo was raised by a single mom and my parents were divorced, so we decided that if and when we had kids we wanted to be married and be that family foundation for our kids. After I had Kiyan, getting married became more of a priority for Melo.

Some people say that marriage today is played out, that it's overrated. If that's the case, then why are so many people fighting so hard to do it?

I had even convinced myself that it wasn't a big deal. But I can honestly say that after having my baby, things changed for me. Marriage became a big deal. I knew I couldn't stay the "perpetual fiancée."

So how do you move from shacking up to marriage? Sometimes you don't. So should you live together first? There are some pros to living with him first. Living with him, you get to see his habits, and you can decide whether he is actually someone you want to be with every day. Living together and dating are much different.

I always say that when you're dating, you're meeting his representative. You're not meeting the real man. When people are dating, everyone's on best behavior and most people are simply wearing masks. But if you live together, it's much harder to keep up the fake persona. You get to see the real him (and he gets to see the real you, too).

One of the cons about living with him first is that he

gets too comfortable. He doesn't feel like he has to move on marriage, and perhaps he will even take you too much for granted. I definitely started feeling this way as the years between our engagement and our actual marriage started rolling along.

I didn't plan on moving in with Melo. It just sort of happened. I was visiting him a lot in Denver, as you know, and I just started staying longer and longer. I started leaving stuff there. Then he cleared a few drawers, then a whole closet, and before I knew it I was living there. Then I got pregnant and we were officially playing house. I didn't want to be pregnant and living apart from him. And considering the kind of pregnancy I ended up having, I needed to be near him.

What was crazy about our relationship was that Melo asked me to marry him so early in it. I just knew we would be married within a year or so, but we could never get around to setting a date. And I wasn't the kind of woman to be pushy about it. I figured when he was ready, it would be the right time.

But as a year turned into three, and then to six with a baby, I started looking at myself. I bent the rules on so many things being with Melo—being with a younger man, being with a baller, living with a man, having a child out of wedlock. These were all things I'd said I would never do. With him, I not only bent and broke my own rules, I shattered them.

And now I was in this relationship with a ring and nothing else. There was no reason not to be married. I kept wondering, what was the holdup?

I did, however, learn a lot in those six years between getting engaged and getting married. The first lesson is that no matter how much you want something to happen when you want it to happen, it's not going to happen until it's time. I was ready to get married the day after he proposed. He wasn't. I stayed because I knew he eventually would be ready.

I see women in long-term relationships who push and try to coerce their man to marry them. That will never work. If he's going to do it, he will. If he's not, he won't. So how long should you wait? That's totally up to you. Again, for me, I knew he wanted to marry me . . . eventually. There was never a doubt that it would happen, which made it easier to endure the wait.

But if your man is not even making a move to get engaged after a lengthy period of time, he probably doesn't want to get married. If you want to get married to him, you may need to take a real look at the relationship and make a decision. If you decide to stay in a relationship with a man who has no interest in marrying you, you cannot get mad at him ten years in. That's your fault. Your sticking around all of those years will not change his mind. What it will do is allow him to take you for granted because he's getting everything without having to commit and give up anything.

If you feel as if he does want to marry you, because he's told you that and he's given you a ring, then you can do a few things to move it along. For one, don't make it so easy for him. Remember, men are hunters. Make him work for it. Move out until he's ready. Because as long as you two are doing everything a married couple would do, he's not going to feel pressed to make it official. Again, I questioned if I should have moved in with Melo. And I probably would have established my own residence had I not had such a difficult pregnancy. Once the baby came, with Melo traveling so much, it was just easier for us to be under one roof.

I do believe that living with Melo made our marriage less of an urgent situation for him. When he said he wanted to spend the rest of his life with me, he meant it. And he was getting the exact same experience without having to actually get married. That was my fault.

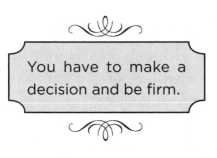

You have to make a decision and be firm.

But if you make the mistake of living together for a long period of time and find yourself perpetually "engaged" the way I was, do not give him an ultimatum. Simply tell him what you expect to happen and if he's not prepared to do it, be prepared to leave or be his girlfriend or fiancée for the rest of your life, or however long it takes.

I didn't want to be the only one in my household with

a different last name. So I sat down with Melo and was straight up about it: "We have a kid. You're grown. I'm grown. And I don't want to play house anymore. We're either doing it or we're not."

You never want to coerce or manipulate someone into marriage. If he wasn't going to marry me, I would have to go, and mean it. Don't *pretend* to do something; it will always backfire. You have to make a decision and be firm.

CHAPTER SEVEN

Game Time:
The Marriage vs. the Wedding

Game time: *Time to go do what has to be done; time to go to work.*

After six years, it was finally happening. We set a date: July 10, 2010. Kiyan was three. We had to do it in the summer because that was the NBA off-season. After a lot of back-and-forth, we decided to have a big wedding—and to have it on television. I was approached by VH1 to film it as part of a reality show. I have heard of people spending ridiculous amounts of money on a wedding, which was something I wasn't interested in doing. It's one day, and while you want it to be memorable, you shouldn't spend a small fortune to show the world that you're married.

So filming our wedding for a reality show seemed like an ideal situation—we would have the big wedding we wanted with our family and at the same time be able to share this special day with the world.

Melo was cool with the taping, but he wasn't okay with them filming every intimate detail of our wedding. My position was either we do it all the way or we don't do it at all. Understanding television, I told him that it wouldn't be right to lead the audience right up to that point and then not give them the whole thing. So we compromised. They got to see some of the vows and some of the partying and reception afterward, but they didn't see all of it.

It wasn't an intrusion because they were literally filming what we were already doing. It wasn't scripted; there weren't several takes of anything. They just rolled the cameras while we did our thing.

Our wedding was beautiful. It was perfect. I couldn't have asked for a more beautiful day. And Melo was into it. He's not the kind of guy to get involved in things like that, but he was totally involved in our wedding, right down to picking the colors. If you look at the film, you'll see a lot of red. That's Melo's favorite color. We even had a red velvet cake. He picked the deejay—DJ Clue, which was perfect, since he introduced us. Neither of us cares about details like that, but this was our day and he wanted it to be right.

It was totally about us.

I walked down the aisle to Kenny Lattimore's "For You," the perfect wedding song. And the reception was just how I like it, free and fun. We have a lot of friends who are singers, and they were grabbing the microphone and belting out songs as Clue spun. Ciara, Kelly, Trina, and Serena even grabbed the mic to sing. I got up there, too. Folks were just being themselves and having a blast. LeBron James, Chris Paul, and Amar'e Stoudemire were there having fun, too. Those personal moments didn't make it on the show. There were quite a few sacred moments that didn't make the cut as well.

To this day, people who were there say that our wedding was like the best party they had ever been to. But when it was all over, when the music stopped playing and everyone went home and it was just me and Melo and Kiyan, I knew that the party we had was fun, but the marriage and us being a family was what it was really all about.

I know some people put so much attention into the wedding that they forget about the marriage. I was mindful of that. We could have done it in front of the justice of the peace and I would have been just as happy. We waited so long that at the end of the day, I couldn't have cared less about the wedding. It was Melo who said, "Let's do it correctly!" and it turned out to be this big bash of a wedding.

It wouldn't have mattered to me either way. A lot of people just show up to weddings for the meal and to gossip:

"Ooh, look at that dress!" They don't even really care about you and your marriage.

I know some people that are more concerned about their wedding and how it looks. The whole Bridezilla thing is real. Driving people crazy over the dumbest things. Some women (and men) really do lose sight of what it's all about. If your wedding sucks, you can still have a great marriage. And you can have a perfect wedding and a disaster of a marriage.

I have seen people spend all of their money on these elaborate weddings, with doves and Rolls-Royce limos and the over-the-top catering, and in less than a year the marriage is finished.

The magic should not be about getting married. The magic should be in *staying* married.

I don't know a lot of people who are married. The landscape of life has changed, and it seems as if marriage doesn't really hold an important place in society anymore.

There was a time, probably my mom's generation, when getting married was a major accomplishment. But people measure accomplishments differently today. I don't know if that's good or bad; it's just the way things are. It used to be if you weren't married by a certain age something was wrong with you; people would talk about you. Today, you can be single and no one cares. There's no pressure or importance placed on marriage anymore. People are opting to travel, focus on their careers, live their own lives.

I'm married. I happened to find someone I wanted to spend the rest of my life with. But if I had never met Melo and I was just dating and didn't have a kid, I think I would be okay with never getting married. I think it's more than okay for a woman to want to do so many things in her life that marriage isn't a priority. There are plenty of women who are satisfied being self-fulfilled. They don't need marriage to feel validated as a person.

Getting married didn't make me feel validated as a person. I was already validated in myself. But it was important for me to do it. It was important for my son to see his parents in a functional relationship. Kids start asking questions very early. I didn't want to be a baby's mother. I needed to be a wife, Mrs. Anthony, mother of Kiyan Anthony.

What's different when you get married?

A lot of things didn't change. But there was this place inside me that had nothing to do with anyone else and that shifted. I'm his *wife*. Your swag is different when you're a wife. People lie when they say wives don't get treated differently than girlfriends. I was now Mrs. Anthony, not the girlfriend or the five-year fiancée. The dynamics within the relationship didn't change, but the dynamics outside it certainly did.

As soon as we went on our honeymoon in Costa Rica and the hotel concierge said, "Welcome, Mr. and Mrs. Anthony . . ." Wow! I had never heard that before.

My mom said when you got married there is so much more riding on it. When you say "I do," you go into your house together. Marriage was different back during my mom's time. It meant starting a whole new chapter. People were waiting until marriage even to have sex during my mom and grandmother's era.

I don't know anyone who is waiting to have sex before marriage. I did hear that DeVon Franklin and Meagan Good waited until they were married. That's the only case I've ever personally heard of. Ever. And I think that's amazing. You don't see people with old-school values, waiting until they're married, anymore. I totally respect that. It speaks to a certain commitment to each other that you just don't see these days.

I love being married. No matter what, I know I have one person in my life who will be in my corner—in sickness, hurt, disability, through financial issues. It's in the vows. We pledged that to each other and God and we both took it seriously.

I know I have someone I can rely on for the rest of my life. How amazing is that? That's the beauty of marriage, knowing you have a partner to be by your side during the difficult times and during the amazing times. That's a partnership.

When I go to bed, even those times when Melo pisses me off and we're arguing, I know he has my best interest at heart. I know that he's looking out for me, that he's protecting me. That he will give me good advice without jealousy or ulterior motives.

That's the real joy in being married.

CHAPTER EIGHT
Salary Cap: His, Yours, and Ours

Salary cap: 1. A maximum limit on salaries. 2. An upper limit to the combined salary of an entire team.

"When should you talk about money in a relationship?"

Very early. Even before you get too serious. They say the majority of marriages fail because of fights over money. So why wouldn't you talk to him about it, hash out where you both stand on the subject, before you get serious? Why wait until you run into money troubles?

I think it's important to manage your expectations about money because you have to know that money comes and goes. So though I was marrying a man with money, I made it very clear that I would have my own back and his if he ever needed me to, because we were a team and I was with him for both of us to win. I was going to respect his pockets. And I was going to respect my own and not rely on him to take care of me.

This is why I'm not a huge fan of prenuptial agreements. To me, it sets your marriage up for failure from the beginning because it's basically saying, "If we break up, I don't want you taking all of my money." Well, why would you marry someone who you think would do that to you? I know things happen and people change and things can get crazy, but to me it just seems like you're placing a built-in "I don't really trust you" clause into your marriage vows.

That's just me. But I do see the other side. I do understand why some men have to protect their money like that. It's a thin line when you're talking about so much money.

I had been around rich people before I got with Melo. I even had a few rich friends. But there's a difference between going to a party at Diddy's house and being blown away by all the opulence and actually *living* in Diddy's house and having that be your life.

Moving to Denver was like that for me. I played it cool. But there were a few "Oh, damn!" moments.

Melo's house in Denver was ridiculous. He had a basketball court in his house—a real hardwood basketball court like you'd see at one of the arenas. He had a lake—an entire lake—in his backyard.

There were rooms in his house I hadn't even been in—it was that big. He had a full-time chef. That didn't take long for me to get used to, because I'm not a great cook. To be able to have someone prepare whatever you'd like at a moment's notice was just dope.

Melo would have a masseuse come over every day, and every ache and pain or sore muscle would be attended to. He was very valuable to the city of Denver. If he coughed wrong, the whole city would be in an uproar and someone would run to make sure he was okay.

It was a different life. I would always think how hard it must be to maintain the connection to the real world. I used to ask him how he stayed in touch.

"How does it feel to never have to worry about money?" I asked him.

He just shrugged.

When I was younger I used to say, "When I get money I'm going to get a penthouse in New York overlooking the park." I had this grand idea of what having money looked like. But when I finally got to the point where I could buy that penthouse, my priorities had changed. It's way more important that I have a stable home, not a nice house. It's more important that I have a loving relationship than expensive things.

Having money—after a while the thrill of it wears off. You may not take things for granted, but it takes a whole lot to be impressed. In fact, very little impresses me today, which is why it's so much easier for me to focus on people's character.

For Melo, money wasn't a thing. He had it. But I had to remind him of the number of NBA players who had it and ended up broke. Whether you're making $20,000 or $20 million a year, if you're spending more than you're making you will end up broke. It sounds simple, but I've seen it happen way too often to not say anything.

So, early in our relationship, I would say, "Babe, do we really need to fly private?" I didn't make an issue of it; I just asked a question. Today we primarily fly commercial. As a partner or spouse, you're there to look out for and help your mate. You're there to make sure you have his or her back. But I've seen relationships where it seems as if the woman or man is out to get their partner. They will either watch them do reckless things with their money and say nothing or worse, they will spend the money and put the entire family behind the eight ball.

I know how hard it is to earn money. Even if it's millions, the work that goes into it is way too much to squander it.

It's so important that you and your spouse are on the same page financially. Just as it's important for the two of you to be physically and emotionally compatible, you have to also be financially compatible. If you're a crazy spender and he's a crazy saver, then you may run into trouble, or you may be the perfect match if you're both okay with the other's habits. If you're spending more than he's making—or vice versa—and it's putting your family in the hole, there will definitely be some issues.

One solution that I believe helps keep a relationship at peace as it relates to money is having His, Hers, and Ours accounts.

He should have an account from which he can buy anything he wants. You should have your account to buy what you want. And you should both contribute to an "Ours" account for the household and the kids.

Marriage shouldn't feel like you're locked down. It's a partnership, not a prison sentence. So if he has his own account from which he can buy whatever he wants, you shouldn't be involved in it or comment about his purchases. If he works every day to earn that money, I don't believe you should tell him how to spend it—as long as he's contributing fairly to the "Ours" account.

And I never want to be in a position to have to ask anyone for anything. If there's a pair of shoes or a bag or even a car that I want, I should be able to get it. I don't expect a man to understand why a woman would wait two months for a shoe to come out. But some of us do. And we shouldn't be scrutinized or asked "Why do you need that?" or told "That's too much for a pair of shoes!" if it's something we want and we've worked hard to afford it. So make sure you have your own account, so you don't have to worry about that. Save up for the things *you* really want.

Some women seek only the money that a man may have and pay no attention to whether or not that man is a good man or even if he actually loves them. If you marry or get into a relationship with a man for his money, you deserve whatever comes with that.

I believe every woman should have her own money and account. For me, having my own money is a form of freedom. It allows me to make decisions and do things freely without depending on or waiting for someone else to weigh in. I'm not saying that in some "I don't need a man!" sort of way. That's not me. Using independence as a weapon—as some women do—is not cool. Knowing you have your independence to fall back on, however, is very cool. It's not just cool for you; it's cool for the relationship.

I have a friend who was married to an NBA player. She never worked while he was playing. He wasn't a star, but a solid player. A couple of years after he left the league, they fell on hard times. All the money, the houses, the cars—it was all gone. That lifestyle that she had grown accustomed to disappeared and she had nothing. *They* had nothing and had to file for bankruptcy.

If she had been working during those years when things were going well and saving her money and building herself and her own wealth, when bad times hit, she could have been there to help pick up the family.

I know that sometimes men with money don't want their women to work. If that's the case, then you have to be smart about the money that does come through your hands. You have a personal "just in case" fund for yourself, for your family, and even for him.

Marriage is a two-way street and just because your man is a great breadwinner doesn't mean you shouldn't participate. Even if the money you make can't compare to the money he makes, it's something. And it gives you a career or something to do or to fall back on.

Wouldn't be it nice to know you have both of your backs? At the very least, you know you can take care of your kids and yourself if, God forbid, something were to happen to him. But even more than the financial security, I think a woman having her own—career, money, etc.— gives her the confidence to be in a relationship because she *wants* to be in that relationship, not because she *has* to be.

I know a lot of women who feel trapped because they have nothing without their man. So they stay in a relationship where they are treated like crap and they put up with things because they don't want to give up their "lifestyle." That's not healthy.

I watched my mother pick up and leave a comfortable situation with nothing—not even a place to stay—and we were a happier family for it. I know firsthand that money really can't buy you happiness. If anything, it can become a crutch that keeps you miserable because you think you can't be happy without it.

When a woman allows a man to totally take care of

her, she leaves herself open to being mistreated. It gives the man too much power in the relationship, and not all men handle that well. Sometimes a man will use his money as a weapon or a tool to control a woman. But if a woman is making her own money, he can't do that.

Melo isn't that kind of man, not at all. In fact, he's laid-back and generous almost to a fault. He loves taking care of Kiyan and me. He would be fine if I decided I didn't want to work. He wants me to be happy. But I know if I'm going to be happy I have to work. It makes me happy to be independent. And it feels good to know that the foundation of our relationship has absolutely nothing to do with how much money he has.

Ever since I can remember, I always wanted to buy a house. I was married when I was finally in a financial position to get the kind of house I wanted. I had been spending a lot of time in Los Angeles working and I was tired of staying in hotels. I found myself out there for weeks and some-times months at a time. When you're in one place for so long, you want to sleep in your own bed.

I also knew that if I ever bought a house it would prob-ably be in L.A. It's so different from New York and Atlanta. L.A. is like my chill place. I can be laid-back and relaxed there. I could also see myself eventually settling there, like my retirement spot.

New York is great. I'm from New York. There are so many things to do in New York, and it keeps you prepared for whatever the world has to throw at you. It's nonstop, fast-paced, and it can be hectic. L.A. allows me to refocus and recharge.

When I was looking at houses, I got some recommendations on properties from a Realtor I knew. It took us less than a month to find the right place in the right location. I'm the type of person that when I see something I like, I know it and I don't need to keep looking. And I found the perfect place in West Hollywood. It was the right size and the right price. I didn't want anything too expensive because I was buying this house, not Melo. I also wanted to make sure that I could afford it. Things happen. You have to always be prepared for the worst. And my worst would be buying a house that was crazy expensive. Yes, right now I have money, but what about ten years from now if the work isn't coming in? Again, I wasn't buying this place for my husband to pay for. This was something I was doing for myself. So I stayed in my financial lane. I didn't want to be in over my head.

I found a nice three-bedroom in West Hollywood. I picked West Hollywood because it reminded me of New York. There are restaurants and shops that you can walk to. And the community is diverse. You have blacks, whites, Hispanics, Asians, and gays. It's a good mix.

It was an older house that the previous owner had torn

down and rebuilt. It wasn't over-the-top or extravagant. I have a room for Melo and me, a room for Kiyan, a guest room (for when Mom visits), and a backyard. There's a cabana area, which is like my outdoor club, where I spend most of my time with friends barbecuing and watching TV. It's like being away on vacation right in my own backyard. It is a very nice house and it meant a lot to me that I was able to buy it on my own.

And I had the support of my husband, who knew this was a dream of mine. He didn't even need to see it before I bought it.

"I know I'm going to love it. Do your thing!" he told me. He was so supportive. That's important, that your man supports the things you want to do. He shouldn't feel threatened because you spend your money on something you want.

My buying this house was all about me accomplishing something that I had wanted to do for a very long time. It was a place I could call my own that I can take full responsibility for. It was also an investment.

Buying my own house was also a major step for me psychologically. But so was going back to work after I had my baby. There were so many people urging me to just stay home and be a mom and not work. And clearly I could have done that. But I've been working most of my life. It's what I do. And in entertainment if you "take a break" you will find that there may not be any work waiting for you when you decide you want to return.

But when I got the call several weeks after I had my baby and was asked if I would consider hosting a reunion show for *Flavor of Love*, I couldn't imagine leaving home to work at that moment. My baby was about a month and a half old and we hadn't spent one day apart. But then I thought about it: What if I didn't get another call? Would I be happy being a stay-at-home mom? I had my manager reach out and tell them I would do it. Working makes me happy. Having my own income makes me happy. I definitely wanted to get back to things that I loved and that made me happy. I didn't want to sacrifice my career because now I had a baby. I don't knock women who do that . . . if that's what makes them happy.

I'm not saying it was easy going back to work after having Kiyan. I cried because I was leaving him for the first time. While I would only be gone for a day, I was torn up. I flew to L.A. from Denver to do the show, and my mom stayed with Kiyan. I was glad I did it, because doing that show opened up more opportunities.

I was ultimately happy.

I make fake comments like "I wish I was rich!" I often joke with my friends and family about the things I would get if I had money. In my mind, Melo is rich. I do very well. What he has, he's earned. That's *his* money. I don't necessarily count his money as my money even if he does. I don't make $20 million a year. I know I can ask him for whatever I want, but there's a great feeling in being able to provide for myself.

I've always hated asking for anything—even as a kid.

"Ma, can I get some money to go to the movies?" I hated asking. So I got a job so I wouldn't have to. That's just the way I've always been. Even before I worked at the radio station, Dice and I worked at Baskin-Robbins together. I also had a job at the Limited, a clothing store. I even worked two jobs at one point because while it was cool getting a ride to school, I wanted my own car and I didn't want to ask anyone to get me one. I never wanted to hear "Not today," or "Maybe tomorrow." And then you're waiting around for someone to decide whether they will give you something you've asked for. Or worse, you ask for something and the response is "You don't need that . . ." If I want it badly enough, I'll either save up for it or I'll go without. Or I will dip into my savings and get it. There's freedom in that.

My first car was a Jetta, a beat-up blue Jetta. I needed it to work at the radio station because it was forty-five minutes from my house and there was no way I was taking a bus to that dicey area near the airport at the times I was working. And I didn't want to depend on anyone to drive me. My mother was doing enough, getting on her feet after her divorce from my stepdad and our move from New Jersey to Atlanta. I didn't want to be a burden to anyone.

Now that I've built a career and have my own financial independence, my mother wants me not to work so much. She wants me to stay home, cook, and take care of my family. She's old-fashioned. I understand where she's coming from. But I see my role in taking care of my marriage and my family differently. This is the way Melo and I have been since we got together. He met me working on television, having my own apartment, with my own car. He fell in love with an independent woman. So why change?

HALFTIME

....

How Do *I* Snag a Baller?

Believe it or not, I get asked this question a lot. So I thought I'd take halftime to answer. The best way to snag a baller is to not make that your goal. For me, it happened organically.

It seems that more and more women set their sights on getting with a rapper, an athlete, or an entertainer—someone who they believe will take care of them financially and give them the kind of lifestyle they see on television and in the movies. When they're looking for a man and to get into a relationship, this is their only goal.

The lifestyle looks really great from the outside—all the money and the fame and all that comes with it, like the free swag and front-row seats to games and concerts and hobnobbing with the rich and fabulous. But . . . there is a whole other side to this life.

I have to say that being in a relationship with someone famous has been one of the most challenging relationships for me. Along with all the wonderful things you have access to, there is an equal amount of shit you have to eat. (I'll get to this in another chapter.)

Here's another truth: Most women who make

snagging one of these high-ticket men their primary goal don't get him.

Yes, he'll sleep with you. He may even have a baby with you, but he won't *be* with you—not the way you may want. He's not taking you home to meet his mother, and it's highly unlikely that he'll put a ring on your finger.

Instead of worrying about what your man is going to do for your social life or what he's going to buy you, look for someone who is going to be a good man, who you can build a solid friendship with, and who wants the same things in life that you do. You will be much happier in the long run if you're with someone for those reasons instead of for the number of zeros in his bank account. And if you're out there being true to who you are and making genuine connections, you never know who you'll attract.

CHAPTER NINE

Training Camp:
The 60 Day Challenge

Training camp: A place where people live temporarily and learn or develop their skills in a sport.

I follow the rapper Game on Instagram (which is my way of staying up with some of my friends when I'm too busy to call). He posted photos of this 60 Day Challenge he was doing and I watched him transform his body. Other people started doing it with him and they were seeing great changes not just in their bodies but in their lives as well. I got inspired by some of the testimonies.

I was in New York and was scheduled to be in Los Angeles in a couple of weeks, so I reached out to Game and told him I wanted to do the challenge. When I landed, I texted him and he told me to meet him at a local café.

"When?" I asked.

"Now," he said.

Dice and I showed up, and he ordered us egg whites and some vegetables and said, "You start today!"

What? There was no warming-up period, no couple of days to get used to the idea. I hadn't even had my chocolate fix that day! This was going to be Day One of my 60 Day Challenge? *Damn!* No fried foods, no alcohol, only fresh fruits and veggies, protein drinks, and skinless, boneless chicken or fish for the next sixty days.

I went through the sixty days, and by the end I was in the best shape of my life. I learned a lot about myself mentally as well as physically. You can go online and check it out for yourself. But what I also learned is that the principles I applied to getting into mental and physical shape in my life could also be applied to my relationship, which I actually did.

Sixty-Day Relationship Challenge (For Those Already in a Relationship)

Is your relationship perfect? Neither is mine. So after my 60 Day Challenge for my body, I decided to do a relationship challenge. My thing is complaining. So I decided not to complain for sixty days. I couldn't believe how hard it was to stop doing it. But I also realized how much time I actually spent in my relationship nitpicking about petty things that really didn't matter. Not doing it made a huge difference in our relationship. We both were happier in the end.

If you're not a nagger or complainer, then I'm sure there's something you do that he wishes you would stop doing. You should also add a few things that he would love for you to do that you don't do frequently enough in his opinion. It could certainly be sexual, but it doesn't have to be.

You can also start doing some nice things for him over the next sixty days. Leave him handwritten notes telling him how proud you are of him and how much you love him every single day for the next sixty days. Fix him a special meal. Or do something spontaneous and unexpected, like give him a bubble bath once a week for the next sixty days.

And don't tell him about the sixty-day challenge. Just do it. And watch how he reacts. Sometimes in a relationship it's easy to take each other for granted. Or we want him to always make the first move and do things for us. Make up your mind that for the next sixty days it doesn't matter what he does or doesn't do; you're going to be the one to either stop doing things that get on his nerves (like nagging) or come up with new ideas and ways to make him happy.

And when the sixty days are over, reevaluate. What

The best things come when you're not looking.

worked and what didn't? You may want to go back to nagging and complaining because that's what he responds to, or maybe you won't have to when the sixty days are done.

Sixty-Day Relationship Challenge (For Singles)

If you aren't in a relationship, the sixty-day challenge is even better. This is a time to focus on you. Pamper yourself. Improve yourself. Get real with yourself. If you're alone and you don't want to be alone, take a break from trying to find Mr. Right. It's probably exactly what you need.

So spend the next sixty days NOT looking, thinking, or trying to get a man.

I've heard a million times from friends and others, "It wasn't until I was happy with myself that all of these great things began to happen to me." That seems to be the formula. It used to sound so corny to me, but it is very true. The best things come when you're not looking.

"If I'm not looking, how am I going to find him?" I've been asked.

He'll find you. Trust me. When you're looking, most of the time what you'll attract is the wrong kind of man. If you're thirsty or desperate, it comes across. So what you'll get is a man who will prey on a desperate woman, not a man who will be the man of your dreams. You tend to attract what you are.

So spend the next sixty days being the woman you want to be. Maybe you need to lose weight. I can tell you for a fact, the 60 Day Challenge will help you to do that. Maybe you just want to get healthier. Or maybe you want to get into shape and start a workout regimen.

Maybe your goals are mental. Find two or three good books and finish them within the sixty days. And make sure they are books that will improve your mind or your spirit. Don't go for the cheesy romance novel. That's not really going to improve your life, is it? Or make it a goal to read the newspaper every day. Like I learned from my stepdad, it can help you in so many ways to be up to speed on current events and build that mental capacity.

At the beginning of this challenge, set some reasonable goals for yourself and then work every day to achieve them. Keep a journal so that you have a reminder of what you were able to do during this period, the places where you struggled, and how you overcame and pushed through.

And start today.

When you're doing this challenge, remember to have fun. Get out there and do some things you've never done before. How is your potential Mr. Right going to see you if you're locked away in the house? Mix it up. My mom used to say, "Prince Charming isn't going to ride up to your door and knock." You have to be out there, just not out there being thirsty and looking desperate. He'll see you when you are looking and feeling your best and being happy.

In order to be in a healthy relationship, you have to be a whole and healthy person yourself. If you spend time working on yourself, you'll be surprised at how much people will start to notice you and what you're doing. And that guy who is out there waiting for you is now getting a complete person.

Keys to Success

One of the things that got me through my sixty days was having a support system. I could go online and see what other people were doing, but I also had physical encouragement.

Every day we'd do a hike, jog, or run up Runyon Canyon, which is this hilly trail in the park in Los Angeles. We had this motto: Nobody gets left behind. No matter what. And I appreciated it on those first days when I could barely finish the trail. I was last a couple of those days, but someone was there with me, pushing me, making sure I finished when I wanted to quit.

By the end of the sixty days, I was one of the people going back to make sure that people finished and didn't quit. Folks would be crying and breaking down, but nobody got left behind.

That should also be applied to your relationships. Sometimes you can find yourself way ahead of your partner or mate and you may just want to run ahead and not look back. But this is a partnership. You can't just leave him behind. If he fails, you fail. So go back and get him, push him, drag him if you have to. Encourage him and be there for him, if he's truly the man you want to be with.

What I also learned is that when you're going through something tough, it's best not to go it alone. You need people to lean on, people to talk to, people to talk you off the ledge when you're thinking about jumping.

That was what the challenge was for me. I had these people there making sure I got through it. And these people became my friends. We shared things no one else could understand because we were all going through the same exact experience together.

In Los Angeles we had a big, tight-knit group. When we were done, Game rented out a hookah bar and we had a blast together, celebrating our shared accomplishments.

Having a challenge or a goal like the 60 Day Challenge allows you to hit the reset button on your life. It's a chance for a new start.

I also learned that it's okay to fall. During the challenge, I had a day where I binged on KitKat bars (chocolate is my weakness). I can't tell you how many of those things I ate. But I felt really bad about myself. I shared this with a few of my 60 Day buddies and they encouraged me to start fresh the next day. Forgive myself. Put it behind me. Move forward.

Sometimes we fall off and we just keep falling. In life we may hit a bad patch and we allow it to overtake our whole life. That bad patch becomes a bad month, a bad year, and then a bad life. Stop at the patch. Hit the reset button and move on.

The other thing we have to watch out for is self-sabotage. We have a tendency as women to do that. When I finished my sixty days, as I said, I was in the best shape of my life. I was feeling really good. But after about a month, I completely spiraled out of control. I started binge eating and stopped working out. What was crazy was that I had a movie to do. Here I had gotten into the best shape of my life, I completely undid all that work, and I now had to be in front of a camera.

I was working on the sequel to Steve Harvey's *Think Like a Man*. And when I see myself in that movie, all I'm thinking is how I messed up. I love the movie, but I hate how I look. I did all that work to prepare for that film and then I did this to myself: craft services, chocolate chip cookies every day while I waited to shoot the next scene, sitting around, not working out.

I did it knowingly. It's crazy. I have an all-or-nothing personality. While I was doing the challenge, I was all in, determined to finish, determined to succeed. And I did. When it was over, I guess I was like, "I did it, it's done, now back to my normal behavior."

But what I also learned is that you need balance. It can't be all or nothing, because few things are. And in relationships you can't go all out and when things don't go the way you want, pull all back and give nothing.

I've learned that even on that sixty-day challenge, you should mix it up. You don't have to work out every single day. Take a day off here and there. Have a cheat day, where you eat whatever you want (okay, maybe not in a relationship!). They say slow and steady wins the race, right? I'm learning that it's okay not to be so extreme. I have to make a conscious effort to create this balance in my life. And that, too, has helped my relationship, because I'm not so intense. And again, when you're feeling off your game, reach out and get help.

But just as important as it is to have support, make sure you eliminate the negativity and the people who will discourage you from completing your goals. In fact, don't even tell them what you're doing.

I was nervous about doing the 60 Day Challenge because I was very public about it. I was posting stuff on Twitter and Instagram. That could have gone either way for me. I felt pressure to make sure I completed it because everyone was watching, but I also had the possibility of the haters saying things to discourage me.

That's why it's so important that your inner circle, the folks who are close to you, are there to support you and have your back to keep you on track.

There's nothing like good friends.

CHAPTER TEN

My Starting Lineup:
Keep Your Friends Close . . .

Starting lineup: An official list of the players who will actively participate in the event when the game begins. The players in the starting lineup are commonly referred to as starters. The starters are commonly the best players on the team at their respective positions.

I believe a key component of being in a healthy relationship is making sure you have a solid team around you. My team, my starting lineup, is made up of my close friends.

This friendship thing can be tricky. Sometimes you can have too many friends, which gives you too many voices in your head and too many opinions. Sometimes you can have the wrong kinds of friends or think you have friends when what you really have is frenemies—people posing as friends who are really there to pull you down. Either scenario can ruin a potentially good relationship.

That's why it's important to pick a solid starting lineup in your life. Who will be there in the trenches with you and who deserves to be there? You should examine your life and the people you have chosen to be in it and ask yourself, "Are they there because they truly care about me and my happiness?" If your answer is no, then they have to go. They're not worthy to be in your starting lineup. Those friends who aren't there for you will always show you in some way.

I was hanging out with a few of my friends and acquaintances at a restaurant/lounge in Los Angeles. One of them had just gotten engaged. She held out her hand, and I said, "Oh, that's a beautiful ring!"

And another one said, "But it's not as big as yours."

So what? I hate that shit. Ladies, we can praise and support one another without it always being a competition. It's okay to be genuinely happy for someone else's happiness, and there are women who may have a nice life and can

> Ladies, we can praise and support one another without it always being a competition.

still appreciate that you are having a nice life too, and be happy for you.

Women especially need to start acting like sisters and knock off the petty jealousy.

"I wish I had your life!"

I hear this all the time. But if a "friend" says this to me, I'm giving them the side eye. Because your friends— your real friends—don't want to be you, and they aren't even really paying attention to the superficial material things you may have. Because they're riding with you.

I have been very fortunate to have some really great friends. Or maybe I've learned not to tolerate fake-ass jealous women in my life. I think of my friends as you would a starting lineup on a team. These are the people you go to when you're in trouble. They're there with you through good times and bad times. With great friends, you can't help but win. In my life, every friend plays a particular role. There are also some friends I may not speak to for years, but they're right there when I need them, and vice versa. There are some I talk to every day. But I can't imagine my life without my good girlfriends.

Friendship is very important to me. My best friend in the whole world is Dice. She is my first cousin, but she's also my better half. She's actually more than my best friend. She's more like my sister. She's known me my entire life. So when I go to her for advice, she can take me way back to all the bad decisions and mistakes I've made in my life and remind me never to make those mistakes again. She also keeps me grounded. She often tells me, "Look how far we've come. Look how blessed we are." She is my connection to my roots and my humble beginnings. It's good to experience new and exciting things with her because she'll say, "Can you believe your life?" and it makes me appreciate it more and not take a thing for granted.

Then there's Po. It seems like Po has been in my life forever. She was a friend of a roommate I had in New York. When I moved back to New York from Los Angeles, MTV put me up in corporate housing for thirty days in Manhattan. A friend of mine from Atlanta moved to New York, and we ended up getting a place in Edgewater, New Jersey. It was a super-cool place to live and it was nice to split the rent and save some money. Some people from the industry, like Fabolous, lived in my building. I saw him all the time. That was the building for the up-and-comers. If you had arrived, you lived in an apartment on the water or in Alpine, NJ, where Eddie Murphy and folks like that lived.

Just about every morning on my way out, I'd see Po sleeping on our couch. At first I was kind of pissed. I was like, "Who is this chick on the couch I paid for?"

After a few months, I got used to her. Then my friend decided to move back to Atlanta. Things weren't working out in New York career-wise for her. And Po just stuck around. On my couch. I didn't have the heart to kick her out. Her family was in Houston. She didn't really have a place to go. Her family was very religious and they didn't approve of her lifestyle.

She was so bold and out there. And I was the exact opposite. She and my cousin became fast friends and she helped Dice really become more comfortable with who she is.

It was Po who introduced the "No judgment" mantra into our circle She would share some of the most outrageous stories with us and would end them with "No judgment!" It opened the door for all of us to feel free to express our deepest thoughts and secrets and know that none of us would face any scrutiny, side eyes, or judgment.

It's important to have a safe place where you can discuss things and not feel like someone is going to judge you. Po set the tone for that in my life.

Po and Dice have been on my reality show from the beginning and I love watching them grow and find their way. For me, being successful means seeing ing my friends successful and happy too. Po is working on a music career, and she and Dice are hosting club dates and standing on their own two feet. What's the point in being

> It's important to have a safe place where you can discuss things and not feel like someone is going to judge you.

successful if you can't lend a hand to your friends? I'm not talking about giving people stuff. I see that a lot with entertainers and athletes. They give their friends from their old neighborhood "jobs," and really all they're doing is buying them stuff and they're not adding to the game at all. The biggest public example of that was probably MC Hammer, who made so much money but had so many people in his entourage who were just leeching him. And when the money was gone, so were they. They weren't friends. And neither was he, really. A good friend teaches a friend how to fish so they can make their own way.

A good friend will provide a friend with opportunities. On the flip side, if your friend is someone who is successful, you might want to come up with an idea or figure out a way to bring value to the relationship, instead of waiting for him to "hit you off." Or make your dreams known and be willing to work your behind off to make it happen. One of Ludacris's closest friends wanted to be a chef. So Chris paid for him to go to culinary school. His friend was focused and wanted to do it. And he ended up becoming a successful chef.

Every friend in my life plays a certain position. Some overlap and change with time. But I know who I can go to when I need to get some advice or feedback. When I'm down in the dumps or nervous about an audition, I know exactly who to call: Kelly Rowland. I go to her when I need encouragement. I've known her for more than ten years. I interviewed Destiny's Child while I was on the radio in Los Angeles. Kelly and I ended up dating guys who were close friends, and we started spending a lot of time together. When you're with your guy and he has friends that he's close with, you kind of end up becoming friends with his friends and his friends' girlfriends, too.

Kelly grew into being one of my best friends. What makes her a good friend? She has the purest heart. You can't get this girl to say a bad word about *anyone*. It's unbelievable. I've never seen anything like it. You could come to her bitching about someone who was nasty to you and her response would be, "Maybe she was having a bad day today."

Kelly is always looking for that silver lining. You may be having problems with someone and you just want to yell, "No, fuck that! She has a messed-up attitude." Kelly will come back with, "You don't know what went on in her day."

She really believes in the best in people. Kelly is also a romantic who believes in true love. You have people who hate life and have been damaged by previous relationships and are jaded. No matter what Kelly may have been through, she still has a great outlook on life. She believes in genuine people and believes that most people want to do the right thing. She always helps me see the big picture and what's really important. If I complain about being tired, she will remind me how blessed I am to have a career that makes me tired.

I love her outlook on life. It is so refreshing. But Kelly Rowland will not be the person I invite to a pity party. She's not participating. She is, however, someone I call when I need a reality check.

Ciara is another best friend I can call on to get a real perspective on things. She's younger than me, but she is so mature. It's as if she's been here before. She has a wise old soul. One of the things I like about Ciara is that she's very selective about who she hangs around. She keeps her circle of friends very tight, very small. So if you happen to be among that circle, she will love you unconditionally and be there for you forever. And you feel special to be included as her friend.

Ciara is someone who will challenge me and tell me if she doesn't agree with something. She's also the one who will remind me when I'm not being a good friend.

"I'd love to hear from you," she'll text me. "I know you're busy, but let me know you're okay."

With social media, you think you're keeping up with your friends. Through Twitter and Instagram you know just about every move your friends are making and you're following their lives. But you have to pick up the phone or drop in to see your friends every once in a while.

I met Ciara while I was on the radio in Atlanta. She

was new to the industry and her manager was a buddy of mine. She asked if I would help Ciara, take her under my wing.

She ended up being not just talented but a whole lot of fun. She does impersonations and we can act silly together. I love that about her, too.

I get accused of being everybody's best friend or saying I'm friends with everyone. And they say it as if that's a bad thing. But really, my close friends I can name. Aside from Dice, Po, S. Dot, Ciara, and Kelly, there's Wiz, who I've known since the third grade, and there's Serena (Williams). I met Serena through Kelly and we clicked instantly. One thing I admire about Serena is her drive and motivation and how much she puts into accomplishing her goals. It's inspiring, and I try to apply that same mentality to the things I do in my life. I asked her one time how she stays focused and keeps in shape. I know for me, I fall off so often it's not funny.

"I'm always preparing for the summer," she said.

We all gear up in the spring to get that "summer body" ready. But Serena is always preparing for the summer. She doesn't wait until the spring. It's every day for her. Her other thing is, "There's nothing a treadmill can't fix."

While Serena is intense when she's on the court or preparing for a match, off the court she is the life of the party. She loves to dance and have fun and she is hilarious, which most people don't know.

Trina (the rapper) is also in my inner circle. I've known her since high school. Trina's so close with me and my family that she frequently picks up the phone and just talks to my mom and gets advice from her on what's happening in her life. There's Nadia, who I met while I was in college. We call her News because she knows everything that's going on in the world. If you want to know something about anything, from foreign policy to celebrity gossip, News will know it. There's Angie and Sylvia. And Loren. I've only known Loren a few years, but she has become very close to me. At this stage in my life, I don't usually make new friends. It's much harder because you can't really know if someone is down for you because of you.

Kim K. came into my life later, after we were both successful. It's sometimes harder to make new friends when everyone knows who you are. It's hard to know who is real and who isn't. But Kim and I bonded during a very trying time for me.

I was going through something with my son's health that I hadn't shared with many people. When Kiyan was two years old, he was experiencing excruciating pain every time he drank milk or juice. It would usually happen at night, but he would be hysterically crying and complaining that his stomach was hurting him. Everyone had a diagnosis about what it was—too much juice, not enough water, too much milk, maybe he will grow out of it. I knew it was something and that it wasn't just going away. We finally took him to a hospital in Los Angeles known for taking care of children.

They ran a battery of tests, including a scan where they had to fill him up with dye. The whole process was hell. It took four people to hold him down to put in a catheter, and he was crying for me. I felt helpless and I couldn't even stay in the room because I wanted to just scoop him up and take him out of there. But we had to find out what was wrong. Then they had to put him in a machine, a scanner where he had to lie flat and perfectly still. He was so uncomfortable and upset he couldn't keep still. He was only two years old and they had to strap him down. They put him in something that looked like a straitjacket, which broke my heart because he was screaming and crying at the top of his lungs.

When the test results came back, the doctors told me he had a very serious ailment and he would need surgery on his kidney. There was a tube blocked, and all of the toxins were backed up, which was causing the pain. They would have to remove the clogged portion and reattach it.

The doctor told me, "Don't freak out. He'll be fine."

Don't freak out?! I freaked out. He explained the whole process and it seemed simple enough. But my baby was still just a baby and he would have to have major surgery. It was really too much. It was the scariest time of my life. My mom and Melo were there, of course. But we were all just nervous wrecks.

The day of the surgery they gave him something before they brought him in for the anesthesia and he was out of it. He looked up at me and said, "'Bye, Mommy . . ." and it seemed that he was saying, "Please don't let them take me." It was so crazy.

Melo was freaking out in his Melo way, which doesn't show outwardly. But I know him. When he's quiet like that, he's going through it. I went to the chapel for comfort, but that too just kept me on edge. This was the pediatric ward of the hospital and there were so many cards and notes and letters in the chapel from parents who had lost their children, who lost their babies. And I just started crying. I was on my knees, begging and praying.

The surgery took about six hours. When they finally came out, they said it went well. We all rushed in to see him. He looked so out of it. They had my kid on morphine. We were trying to keep it together. While the doctor said it went well, the recovery was worse than the illness. He was still in so much pain, and the morphine drips had him so out of it, it was just hard to watch. Everyone came through—all of my family and friends. Even my dad flew in to visit.

While I was in the hospital, I got a call out of the blue. It was Kim K. And while I wasn't sharing this with people outside our circle, she caught me at a vulnerable moment and I told her what I was going through. We had really only just met. She didn't know me well at all. And I ordinarily wouldn't burden anyone with such heavy news, but it was in the moment.

"Oh, my God!" she said. "What hospital?"

I told her, but I actually didn't want people around me because I didn't want to break down. And I didn't want people there seeing him because he just looked so sick and so bad.

But a couple hours after we hung up, Kim just walked in. I could hear the hospital staff outside the room making a fuss and I didn't know why. Then she comes in, in full makeup and glammed out, straight from filming. She brought food for all of my family and she sat there with us for hours. I mean hours. We left Kiyan's room after a while and went to the McDonald's in the hospital and we sat there and talked for more hours. As much as I felt like I didn't need anybody and didn't want to see anybody, I realized it was a relief to talk with someone who wasn't directly going through it with us.

Of course, all of my friends came to visit and sent food and were there for us, but I had just met Kim. She was new to our lives, and here she was going through this trying time with us and being a true friend. I knew there was something genuine about her. She had never met Kiyan before, but she was there for him. So when I hear people say negative stuff about Kim, I always jump in and say that they don't really know her.

We didn't know if my son was going to make it, and

Kim came to the hospital and sat with us all night. It was a moment when I was like, "Wow!" And we've been friends ever since.

I believe friends—real friends—bring balance to your life. They are there as sounding boards, as support, to share their experiences, give advice. I'm leery of people who don't have genuine friends because I believe it says more about you if you don't.

Another new friend in my life is Loren Ridinger. She is someone who fit into a void I had in my life. And she has become an important person to me as I'm growing in my career and building my empire. She has a billion-dollar company—Market America, an Internet retailer. To watch how she's built this company with her husband from the ground up is inspiring. To see what she's created out of nothing makes me know anything is possible. Loren is a person I can talk to about personal things, but also business matters. I look at her as a sister/mentor, all in one. They say you become like the people you spend the most time with. If I can pick up on Loren's business savvy, I'll be great. It's good to have someone in your life who can guide you in business and those difficult decisions, and who also happens to be a friend. She would do anything for me. I never had that kind of female mentor. I've learned so much from her already: from the way she dresses to the way she handles people. I have learned how to be more aggressive. She taught me that I can't want to be liked so

much. That trait can make me make bad business decisions. "You're running a business, so you have to put your
business needs before being liked." She drills that into me.
I keep people around me longer than I need to because I
have a hard time firing people and saying no.

Melo and I enjoy spending time with Loren and her
husband, J.R., as a group. We've taken trips to Thailand
and Italy together. It's nice to have a couple who have been
together for more than twenty years and are not merely just
functioning but are still in love and making it work. I
didn't know how important it was to have role models in
your life like that until I started spending time with Loren
and J.R.

One season on my show, Tyrese (Gibson) and I got
into it. He was coming at me because all of my friends were
single. "What I don't understand about you," he said,
"you're getting married and all your friends are single. You
need some married people around you." I didn't agree with
him. I felt you didn't have to be married to understand it.
But now as I've gotten older, there is a different dynamic to
being married than even being in a long-term relationship.
And it's definitely different from dating.

It's so awesome to talk to another couple about life,
their marriage, and conquering the world and business,
and to do so with your husband. Melo and I never really
hung out with married people before. It wasn't on purpose;
we just never knew any married couples we wanted to hang

out with. Except for News and her husband, P. Stew. They are our very own Will and Jada. They've been together so long. And it's like a honeymoon phase for them 24/7. They live in Maryland and we live in New York and L.A. But we talk all the time.

News is someone who saw me grow into where I am now. She was around when I first met Melo. And she gave me one piece of marriage advice that she is adamant about: Don't be afraid of marriage counseling. That was something I would never even consider. News said that you go through different phases in your marriage and you have to be willing to get help when you need it. That let me know that the road can get rocky, but you have to find ways to work through it.

Sometimes in your life you will have friends who are just there for a season. You may love them and then, for no reason or fault of your own, you just grow apart and stop speaking. I have a friend like that. We were inseparable when I was in Atlanta. To this day, I have never been able to make sense of why we just grew apart. We were so tight in high school. Her nickname was PJ, for Plain Jane, and mine was Holly, for Hollywood. (This was way before I had even thought about

> The road can get rocky, but you have to find ways to work through it.

moving to Los Angeles. People just saw me this way.) We were so close that I tattooed our nicknames on my leg. We were yin and yang. Opposites who had a lot in common. We both were into music and wanted to be in the music industry. Then we just fell apart. I can't pinpoint when it happened. But I really miss my friend. So much time has passed that I don't even know how to patch it. And we probably won't.

PJ went on to realize her dreams and she became a giant in her industry. I sit in awe of this woman. Everything she said she would do she's done and more. We see each other from time to time at industry events. We hug and we say we love each other and we promise to catch up. But then we go our separate way and never do. Time? Distance? Career? Maybe we're both guilty of not making the friendship a priority at some point. I get sad even today just thinking about what happened to our friendship. And I know it'll never be the way it was. I sometimes wish we had had some sort of blowup so I could make sense of it. But there was no argument, no drama, just distance. It's been a hard pill to swallow for me. She meant so much to my life and my progression during those early years.

We would sit in my room night after night, talking about how we would get to Hollywood. And we both made it. It's unbelievable. I will always be her number one fan even from afar. There's always a special place in my heart for her. Perhaps PJ was my friend for a season. That makes me really sad. I would have never imagined the life I'm living now without PJ in it the way we used to be.

Then I have friends, like S. Dot, who are there for a reason, who are there for certain periods or experiences in my life to help me get through. After my breakup with Doug and my move to Los Angeles, I made a really great friend there who helped me during that transition.

Shanika Clay, who everyone called S. Dot, worked in the sales department at the radio station. We met in the break room where we all ate lunch. We struck up a conversation one day, and it just went from there. She reminded me a lot of myself. She was a hard worker, not fazed by the Hollywood lifestyle, and tight with her family. She lived with her mom. I would stay at their place some nights after the club because I didn't want to go back to my empty apartment.

She grew up in Inglewood and knew her way around. She took me under her wing and we would go to clubs together. She let me know the cool places to go in town, and also the places that I should avoid. She introduced me to parts of the city I wouldn't even have known existed.

S. Dot understood some of what I was going through. She shared some of her heartaches, and we connected. Our friendship happened naturally. God knows I needed a friend, but I wasn't going up to people trying to make friends.

I was cautious when I came to L.A. After my mother

left, it was a bit intimidating. People in L.A. are different from people in New York and even those in Atlanta. Everybody in L.A. seemed to want to be in "the business" and it seemed as if everybody had an angle. Waiters were really actors, waiting for their break. Store clerks were models. Every regular working person was really looking to break into movies, modeling, or music. People seemed to want to be your friend to see what you could do to help further their career. So I was cautious. S. Dot, however, was just real.

My radio shift was only four hours, and that left me with a lot of time by myself. I was lonely. I cried a lot. My family was all back east. Everyone I was close to was in Atlanta. I remember thinking, "Wow, is this what being a grown-up is all about?"

I was wishing I had gone on the road with Chris (aka Ludacris). I missed him and Poon.

Then S. Dot would come around and grab me to get something to eat. I would spend a lot of time in Inglewood at her mom's house and I would crash there some nights just not to be alone. I finally found this apartment on my own, which I liked a lot. I brought S. Dot to check it out. She was like, "La, that's like the worst neighborhood you could possibly move into."

When I saw it in the daytime it seemed cool. But I went back at night with her and I saw it was a really bad neighborhood. I guess I drove in and everything was new and beautiful inside the building and I had already given them a deposit. I told them I didn't want it and they kept my deposit. I ended up staying in corporate housing another month.

I was scared as a single girl to be living alone. I didn't know what I was doing and I was mad at myself for losing that money.

Sometimes you get a little embarrassed because you want to be grown and know everything. But you end up making way more mistakes. It's great to be independent. But it's better to have friends that you can bounce things off of and get advice from.

TIMEOUT

·····································

Does He Like Me?

After a great first date with a guy, he's not calling. What does this mean?

This one is easy. If he's not calling, he probably doesn't like you. I know it's harsh. But we sometimes ask questions and the answers are right there. Ask yourself this question: Does he *act* like he likes you?

Guys are pretty simple. They're not that complicated. If they like you, they show you. They may not all do the flowers and call you ten times a day (in fact, most don't). But there are simple things they do to let you know. They will ask you about your day and they will want to know more about your life. But if he isn't calling at all or if you call him and he has a thousand and one excuses for why he can't meet up with you, then he's simply not into you.

I believe after the first date, you don't have to do that waiting-for-him-to-call game. That game is played out. You can make the first move; you can call him first to let him know you had a good time. But after that, if he doesn't appear to make any more moves to see you, let it go.

If you have to do some kind of trick, magic, or voodoo, that's clearly an indication that he's not the one for you. If a man really likes you, you don't have to work that hard. The message of this whole book is to be who you are. You don't have to fit into a mold of what you think he wants. Be you. If that's not good enough for him, then he's not the one.

CHAPTER ELEVEN
The Rules

Rule: 1. A prescribed guide for conduct or action.
2. An accepted procedure, custom, or habit.

As I mentioned in the introduction, you make the rules. So why make them so hard that even you can't play the game? A lot of women today have these goals that they've set for themselves that are making them miserable. My advice: Toss them out and live your life. Don't worry about how it looks or what someone may think.

One of my friends called and said, "I slept with him on the first date. Am I a ho?"

"It depends," I told her. "Do you feel like a ho?"

I've never slept with someone on the first date. I never

even had a one-night stand. But I'm not opposed to it. I've just always been a relationship person. I like being in love. I like having that one person to do special things for. Being a serial dater could never work for me.

That said, I don't believe there is anything wrong with women who are serial daters. But you must know that there is a double standard in our society. If a woman sleeps with a hundred men, she's viewed as a ho. If a man sleeps with a hundred women, he's killing it. He's a hero. He's looked at as a stud and they celebrate him. This is the stereotype, whether we like it or not. So if a woman wants to be that woman who dates a bunch of men, then she better be prepared for the label. It's not fair. It's just the way it is. I stopped trying to figure it out.

But labels and opinions don't matter as long as that woman doesn't view herself as a ho. Who cares? Be you! I happen to know a couple of women who date a lot of men and they don't care how it looks. I applaud them because they're being themselves and living their lives. What I have no respect for are the women who knowingly date other women's husbands and boyfriends. And I don't respect women who pretend to be all pure and chaste and are out there running wild behind closed doors. They're hiding. I prefer someone who says, "I'm going to do it the way the guys do it," and doesn't care what people think.

But if we're being perfectly honest, women can't really do it the way guys do it. Not just because society frowns on it, but because most women aren't wired the way men are wired. We want certain things. And just sex won't cut it for most of us. (There are a few rare exceptions.) But I've found that even women who say they can have sex with a man with no strings attached and just keep it moving end up at some point getting caught out there.

So should you sleep with him on the first date? If you've done it and it's worked out for you, then good. But I will say, more often than not, it doesn't turn out well.

For me, if I'm having sex with you, then we're together. So I need to make sure we're on the same page or my heart will get broken. So not sleeping with someone I like early is my own way of protecting my heart.

Another reason why I don't do it is because I've seen how guys treat women who do sleep with them quickly. I've been fortunate to have a ton of male friends, and they talk honestly with me. I hear how they talk about women who they feel are sluts. But more than that, I watch what they do. The key to understanding men is to observe their actions—how they act speaks volumes.

I recently started taking boxing lessons, and my boxing coach, Mr. Martin, told me that everything is a competition for men.

"Men are natural hunters," he said. "They love the thrill of the hunt. Women don't understand that. So you never want to make it easy for them. They love the challenge."

He wasn't telling me anything I didn't already know, but it was cool getting confirmation. I know we'd like to think there shouldn't be any game playing in relationships. But being in a relationship is very much like playing a big game.

One day you have the upper hand; the next day he has it. But you have to know the rules and you have to learn how to play, or you will end up losing every time.

Sex

Let's talk about sex. What is it really? A connection between two people. A lot of times women allow bad sex to be a deal breaker in a relationship. But what is bad sex? It's a bad connection. Is that something you can fix? Again, get in the game! Show him what you like, how you like it, where you like it. You're in control.

I know a lot of women who are uncomfortable directing a man in bed. It's not what you do but how you do it. You can direct him without being forceful. You can be in control without taking over. If your "direction" still doesn't result in great sex, check the connection. Maybe you guys aren't really clicking; maybe you aren't really connecting. Maybe he's not that into you and is just going through the motions.

But if he were the one, it would be a shame to throw away a good person because of miscommunication in the bed. Do I think sex is important? Of course. But I also think if your guy is a good guy, you can have fun working with him until he gets up to speed. That too takes maturity. I'm kind of shy in this area. I'm not the kind of woman who can easily tell a guy what I like in bed. But if I had an issue and I really liked him, I would. It would be worth it.

Instead, we oftentimes hold a grudge because a man can't read our minds. "Why doesn't he know where to touch me? He must not love me enough. He must not be in tune." Maybe he's just not that experienced. And everybody is different. Maybe the last chick was easy and what worked on her won't work on you. How would he know that? Either you have to either tell him or you have to show him. Trust me, a man wants you to enjoy yourself. So helping him help you do that makes it good for both of you.

Don't assume he should know. If you're not getting what you want in the bedroom, take possession of the ball.

Rule No. 1:
Know What You're Both Playing For.

For you, it may be a long-term relationship. Perhaps your ultimate goal is marriage. For 99 percent of the men you run into, I can almost guarantee you that the ultimate goal is *not* marriage. So you need to figure out what he wants. I'll make it easy for you: He wants sex. But if you give him sex too soon, what does he have left to play for? Where's the challenge? You have to be around him long enough to get beyond the sex and get to know the man and what's at his core. You may find out that nothing is there; he's totally empty. By not sleeping with him you get to dodge a bullet.

But if you believe he is the one and you want him as a husband or a life mate, how do you play it to win?

For me, I can honestly say I didn't come to this conclusion trying to play games. How I behaved was just a natural extension of who I am. I understood that for men—especially men in the spotlight—sex comes easy. Women—beautiful, gorgeous, sexy women—throw themselves at athletes and entertainers every single day. I've witnessed it.

When I was on the radio in high school, my male coworkers and other deejays would have women approach them in the clubs and at the station. (Even our music director had groupies.) The next day I would hear the stories of the conquests. And these were just guys from the local radio station.

I was "one of the boys," so they weren't being disrespectful in talking about these women to me, but I was able to see which girls actually caught my boys' hearts. And she was rarely that chick in the club. She was usually the one he met somewhere who wouldn't give him the time of day. She was the one he had to chase.

With Melo it was a similar story. I was running as far from him as possible when we met. All I could think about was what my stepfather told me: "Don't ever mess with a ballplayer. They are all dogs!" And I can't say my experiences watching friends of mine involved with ballplayers here or there did anything to prove my stepfather wrong. So when Melo and I were introduced, I was not interested. The other factor working against Melo was his age. But I didn't find out about that until I already liked him.

When we did start talking, I never came out and said, "You're not getting the drawers!" I didn't make it an issue. I carried myself in a way that was open and fun and easy to be with. At the end of the night, I left him with a warm hug, a peck on the cheek or lips, and a "good night."

This leads me to . . .

Rule No. 2:
Distinguish Yourself from the Pack.
Be Different.

I'm not talking about tattoos and tongue rings (although some guys are really intrigued by all that). But if you notice all the chicks around you are dressed the same, act the same, talk the same, then you should be the one who is different. If you aren't the "baddest" chick in the bunch who is doing it better than everyone else, what is there about you that stands out?

I've been at the clubs inside the deejay booth and watched the cattlelike dance that goes on as men are on the prowl, and I've seen what they see and what they go for. Of course, in a club men want to bag a beautiful prize. There is no time or space to really get to know someone in a club. So if you do meet a man in a club, please know that he couldn't care less about your personality. And if you give him what he wants (sex), it's likely he'll be gone—unless it's really, really good sex. Then he'll stick around—just for the sex. But that's not a building block for a lasting relationship. That's a building block for a really good sex buddy.

From doing club appearances, I've also watched how women throw themselves at men, especially if that man is in the limelight. A lot of these women have no morals or values. And while a guy will definitely sleep with a woman without morals and values, is he going to bring her home to meet his mother or grandmother or sisters? Is she the kind of woman he envisions being the mother of his children—not his baby's mama, who is essentially a jump-off that he got sloppy with?

Are you the woman he can see having a *serious* relationship with? Do you have the things he's looking for in a wife or the mother of his kids? Do you even know what that man you think you want is looking for in the woman of his dreams?

Male friends of mine have told me that a man knows almost immediately when he's met "the one." The vision for his perfect woman or the woman who would be his wife is something he has been carrying around with him probably since birth, and when he meets her he knows. He knows almost instantly. So if you're with a man for five years or more and he hasn't put a ring on your finger and he keeps running from the very idea of even getting engaged, then you're not the one. He's waiting for the woman of his dreams and you're just holding her spot until he meets her.

You may eventually coerce him into marrying you, but just know that he's settling, thinking that he may not ever meet her. Or maybe he has and he has fucked up with her in some way and can't get her back. You are still his alternative choice. You're not the one. Maybe that's okay with you. But for me, I want to be with someone for whom I am the one. Even if I'm not the one forever or he's not the one forever, at least I can know in my heart that I had that kind of love.

But first you have to believe you are worthy.

Rule No. 3:
Don't Be Afraid to Mess Up or
Go Outside Your Comfort Zone.

What if your first date is a disaster? How do you get a second date? First impressions are so lasting. But if you're convinced that he is worthy of the time you'll spend to get to know him, then you owe it to yourself to give it another chance.

If on that first date you completely made a fool of

yourself or things didn't go the way you thought they should, don't call him immediately. Wait a minute. Collect your thoughts and come up with a plan of action.

My plan of action would be the truth. It usually works. I would call him a couple of days later and say, "I felt like that date was really bad. I was having a crazy day. Do you think we can try this again?"

Simply ask him for a do-over. I think something like that would work. Everyone is entitled to a bad day, and if he's a nice guy, he will definitely give you a chance to redeem yourself. If he isn't a nice guy, why would you want to be with him anyway?

This also falls under the "don't be afraid to make the first move" rule. If you like this guy, let him know. I believe in chivalry and the traditional way of dating. But sometimes guys are just plain scared and too intimidated to make that next move.

Even if you had a great date and he hasn't called you after a day or two, it's okay to pick up the phone to say, "Hello" or "What's up?" It shouldn't be serious and don't ask him, "Why haven't you called?!" Just check in. Tell him you had a nice time. And let him take it from there. If he's not interested, he won't keep the conversation going for long and he won't ask you out again. But you might not ever know that unless you make the first move sometimes.

I was nervous the first time I made the first move. But then I thought, "What do I have to lose? I can either have another date and it can go well. Or he's just not into me. Either way, I'm not losing."

Rule No. 4:
Have Your Own . . . Career, Money, Life.

I've talked a lot in this book about the need to have your own career, your own money, and your own life. There's nothing more unattractive than an insecure woman. And conversely, there is nothing more attractive to a man than a secure, independent woman.

A man will take advantage of an insecure woman. He will definitely sleep with an insecure woman (how easy is that?). But being with her for the long haul?

> There is nothing more attractive to a man than a secure, independent woman.

That's way too much for most men to handle. An insecure woman is also typically jealous and she brings too much drama to every situation. She needs a man's constant reassurance and attention, and keeps asking him dumb questions like "Do you love me?" or "Why didn't you call?"

You are not good mate or good wife material if your whole existence is wrapped up in your man. Initially, a man loves to be the center of your universe. But he doesn't usually want the responsibility that goes with it. So you have to figure out how to make him *feel* like he's the center of your universe while at the same time making sure that *you* are the center of your universe and that you are living your best life.

Men need to feel like the man. And you can do that. Stroke his ego. Put him on a pedestal verbally. But I've found that men are also intrigued when you're doing your own thing and are confident in your life. It is literally a magician's trick I'm telling you to perform, but while you're making him feel like a king, you must be the queen. Don't worry about what he's up to and what he's doing. You need to spend more time working on yourself.

I don't run Melo's phone, check his text messages and e-mails, or spy on him. If I have to do that, then we don't have much of a relationship. My doing that would also say a lot about me. I cannot control a thing he does. But by being fulfilled in myself and in my own space, I can control what I do. So if he does mess up like that, I may be hurt, but my world won't end. And because I'm not obsessed with trying to figure out, watch, and control what he's doing, I don't give myself unnecessary stress. As my mother says, "He's going to do whatever he's going to do." Even if you hire a private detective to follow him, that's not going to stop him. And trust me, the truth always comes out eventually, so why waste the money?

Live your life. Access your value and cultivate your talents and skills. Being beautiful and good in bed just simply isn't going to keep him. There are girls out there who are more beautiful and better in bed and are willing to do *anything*. How do you compete with that? My answer: You don't!

I decided that I was always going to be myself, put it out there, and the one who appreciates what I have to offer deserves to be with me.

Rule No. 5:
Pay Attention! He May Be
There All Along.

Sometimes we work the game so hard that we miss it when there's an easy move right in front of our faces. We're so busy playing, and out there looking to see it.

I know a woman who was so busy with her career that she never could find love—at least that was her excuse. But her true love was right in front of her the whole time and she simply wasn't seeing him.

She and her man had been friends for more than fifteen years. They had been there for each other through several bad relationships on each side. Little did she know he had never gotten married because he was waiting for her. As I said, sometimes men are afraid and intimidated and won't make that move. It took him fifteen years to finally tell her how he felt.

What did she do? She dismissed him. They were friends, she told him. She didn't see him that way.

"I understand," he said. "But if I can't be your man, I can't be your friend. It's too painful. I'd rather move on with my life and try to forget you."

This stunned her, but being a good friend, she let him go. As the weeks went by, though, she discovered that she missed him. A lot. And the more she missed him, the more she started more than just missing him.

"I knew I loved him as a friend," she said. "But when he cut off all ties, I realized that he was more than a friend to me. He was the kind of man I could see spending the rest of my life with. He had all of the qualities I said I wanted, but I just wasn't willing to even give him a chance."

She called him after several months. And before he hung up, she told him, "I think I'm in love with you . . ."

They ended up getting married, and they now have a three-year-old little boy and are happy as can be.

Sometimes what you're looking for is right in front of you. We're so busy looking for that perfect man that we often don't give a guy a chance that might be right there all along.

So take a breather, pause, pay attention.

CHAPTER TWELVE

The Fake:
It May Work in Hoops—
Not So Much in Relationships

Fake: A deceptive move to throw a defender off balance and allow an offensive player to shoot or receive a pass; players use their eyes, head, or any other part of the body to trick an opponent.

They say the way to a man's heart is through his stomach. So what happens if you don't cook? I know several women who either don't cook or hate to cook but faked it in the beginning of their relationships. They put on this whole Suzy Homemaker act because they knew that most men, when they're looking at a woman as wife material, want to see a woman cook, take care of the household, and all of that.

While I believe that men do appreciate a woman who can really rock in the kitchen, I don't believe it is the deciding factor in winning a man's affections. What I know for sure is that pretending to be something you're not will backfire.

If cooking isn't your thing and you're getting the cookbooks out and making these fabulous and impressive meals for your man, can you really keep it up? He will grow used to the great meals and maybe two months or two years into the relationship, when you've decided you can't do it anymore, he's giving you the side eye, like something's wrong. And eventually, something that started off making him feel special will make him feel like you don't care as much, when the truth is you never cared about cooking. It was all a front. It was fake.

As I mentioned before, I don't cook (often). And when I first started dating seriously, I hated cooking. I saw it as a complete waste of time and got no enjoyment out of it. It was so much easier to order out or go out. Melo was fine with it because that's not why he wanted to be with me. He became attracted to me, not to my cooking skills or other things. So now when I cook, it's special.

And over the years, I have not grown to enjoy cooking, because I don't think I ever will be passionate about it. But I have grown to enjoy what having a meal that I've prepared with my family means.

There is a bond that food brings to a family. There is

something about making a meal and everyone sitting down together and eating it. I don't make anything elaborate. I may just cook something simple like turkey burgers and a fruit salad, but I make it just for them. Every now and then I will do the whole spread. That's really something. I also realize that for my son and husband, I want to make some dishes that they will know are special and just for them. Kiyan gets home cooking all the time when he's at my mom's house or my brother's house. But when I make a meal, he knows it's just for him and it's memorable. So I do try to cook at least once a week. But it's not my thing. And if it's not your thing, you should find *your* thing.

Even though I didn't cook for Melo, I brought other things to the table. Of course, he was pretty well known when we got together, but his world was primarily sports-based. I actually knew more people in different industries and was able to bring him certain business connections. For example, he was interested in doing a vitamin drink. I connected him with friends of mine who could help him get the drink not only made but also distributed. When Melo wanted to get his nutrition on track and eat healthier, I hooked him up with my guy Kane, who was an up-and-coming chef. And it worked out wonderfully for both of them.

I don't cook, but I know how to make connections and bring people together. That's my gift. And Melo appreciates it.

You have to find your specialty. Maybe it's giving the world's best massages. Who's to say that a massage isn't as satisfying to some men as a great meal? That massage can mean just as much to him, if not more. If that's your thing, work it. But find *your* thing.

If I came into the relationship doing things that I don't normally do, like cooking, he would expect it all the time. And I simply wouldn't be able to keep it up, or I would be miserable trying. And he would eventually take it for granted. I had to establish that I wasn't going to be cooking early on, and he doesn't expect it.

But I do other things.

A Time to Fake

There are times when you should fake it in a relationship. They say fake it until you make it. In relationships, you can fake it if it means bringing you closer together or opening your world, because you never know.

On my last birthday, Melo surprised me with a trip to Napa Valley. He is a huge wine person and is obsessed with red wine. He rented this beautiful villa overlooking the vineyards. And we spent a day driving to the different vineyards, eating cheese, tasting wines, and getting a lesson on the grapes and how they were grown.

Melo was in heaven. I was not. I felt like I was in a history class and about to die. I don't really drink. I get teased when we go out because I'll order a drink and it will just sit there. I don't like the taste of alcohol, not even the sweet drinks that everyone seems to love. The best I can do is shots because I hardly have to taste the alcohol. I just feel the burn and get the buzz and that's cool. But alcohol is not my thing, and I don't like wine.

I tried to act happy—after all, he went through all the trouble for my birthday—but I couldn't keep up the front. My face said it all. And all I was thinking was, "He knows doggone well I don't like to drink . . ."

"Babe, I don't think you're enjoying yourself," he said.

"Well, wine is your thing," I said. "It felt like you planned something that you liked instead of what I like."

I would have been cool going to Six Flags or to a water park. But me saying that to him hurt his feelings. He felt like I didn't appreciate his effort, and I did. When I thought about it, I got mad at myself. I was being really selfish.

Of course he knew I didn't like to drink. That wasn't what the trip was about. Not at all. But I couldn't see it at the time. Instead, all I saw was that he planned a trip doing something that only he liked. But what he really was doing was opening a part of his world to me. He was letting me in to see why he likes wine so much. This was a bonding trip. And I blew it.

I know I would have been mad had he planned a trip to Napa with a few of his boys who also like wine. Instead, he included me in a world that he loves. Maybe I will never love wine or wine tasting. But how horrible was it really to sit in a villa with a wonderful view, sharing an experience with a man I love? I could have endured those couple of hours at the vineyards with a real smile on my face; after all, we had the whole rest of the day and night to do things I wanted to do.

I ruined the moment by not seeing the full picture. (How many times have we done that?) I should have faked it until I figured it out, instead of just reacting to how I was feeling in that moment. Sometimes we need a ten count in a relationship. We have to ask ourselves a few questions, and the answers would tell quite a different picture. And sometimes we have to react with our head instead of our heart.

CHAPTER THIRTEEN
The Uniform

Uniform: Dress of a distinctive design or fashion worn by members of a particular group and serving as a means of identification.

True to my heart, I am a tomboy. I can get super-glamorous when I have to. But people who know me know it's straight Jordan, straight T-shirt, straight jeans as often as possible. That's my uniform. That's what I'm comfortable in.

You could find me hanging out with Kiyan and his friends, shooting hoops (and yes, I can still take them), and I'm perfectly at home.

When I was in high school, I didn't date much because I was the tomboy, the girl who hung out with the guys but wasn't seen as a girl they wanted to date. I was their homegirl. I liked that designation. But when I did want a boyfriend, I found it hard. And it was all because of my look.

The girls who were getting the boys were wearing the tight jeans, the revealing shirts. They were wearing makeup. I guess I didn't want a boyfriend badly enough, because that seemed like a lot of work. Looking back, I'm glad I was a tomboy and the girl all of the guys liked hanging out with—respectfully. I liked being the only girl in the crowd. It gave me a lot of insight. I also got to learn a lot about men from the inside. And I got to become really comfortable being me. Not changing for anyone.

Being a tomboy actually paid off in the end. Because when I was ready to step out in the revealing dresses, the six-inch heels, and the makeup, I was turning heads and getting that kind of attention. And then I was able to keep their attention. I was the best of both worlds to a guy. They could take me to events and I could look good on their arm when they were out on the town, and I could beat them at video games and talk sports with them afterward.

You know the saying that men want a lady in the street and a freak in the bedroom? I believe they also want a woman who can let her hair down and play, and then put it up and look glamorous when she has to.

Outside of not getting a lot of male attention in high school, I felt good about myself. But when I got to college and started going to clubs with Doug and seeing the girls that were around him, I started feeling differently about my sneakers, T-shirts, and jeans thing. He was originally attracted to my homegirl look, but the girls he was cheating on me with were the chicks in the tight, short dresses. I started questioning myself. But at this point, I wasn't comfortable in tight clothes.

The honest truth is I'm not totally comfortable dressing like that now. I dress up because I have to—mostly for work. But on an off-day, you will catch me without any makeup, with a baseball hat, sunglasses, and *maybe* I'll comb my hair.

From what I hear from Melo and other friends, men like that kind of versatility in a woman. I've had male friends tell me, "I like my chick better when she has on sweats." But I know he also likes it when she dresses up. They like you to be able to do both. Melo always tells me to take off my makeup when I get home from working. He loves it when I'm natural and my hair is pulled back in a ponytail. Versatility is the key.

What's really cool about fashion today is that you can be fly and still be comfortable. Girls are wearing baseball caps and looking fly. It's not like before when you wore caps and sneakers and looked hard. They have caps that are feminine. I love wearing my Nike wedges. Jimmy Choo has sneaker wedges, too. So you can have a feminine look but still hold on to the tomboy in you.

"What Do I Wear on a First Date?"

I get asked this question a lot. My thoughts on the first-date look are to be appropriate and use common sense. If he's taking you bowling, and you show up in ten-inch heels . . . really? Come on! Be realistic. There is such a thing as trying too hard. You want it to look effortless. You might have spent three hours getting ready, but you want it to look like you're just pulled together like that.

You should put effort in your appearance, especially on a first date, because first impressions are important. You don't get a second chance to make a good first impression, so make sure you smell good and you look good. Your clothes should reflect who you are, in keeping with the whole living inside-out theme. But it's okay to throw on a little makeup, even if you don't normally wear it. What that says to him is that you tried to look special for him, and that will make him feel good.

You don't get a second chance to make a good first impression.

Now, to look good on that date doesn't have to break your bank. I follow these girls on Instagram who are so stylish. With Instagram, you can see how others are putting looks together. And there are so many outlets to follow people who know how to get this high-fashion look for less. They mix items from Target or Forever 21 with something more expensive, and the whole outfit looks high end. So you may have on a pair of $100 jeans with a Forever 21 or Target top.

I'm not the greatest fashion person. I'm not creative that way. But I look at some of my favorite people on Instagram and I copy what they're doing. Or I check out a fashion magazine or one of the fashion blogs. They always have articles on how to put together a designer look for less. I rip out something that I think is nice and take it with me when I go shopping. You don't have to be a fashionista to look like one. You don't have to reinvent the wheel. The Internet and social media have made what was once very stressful for someone like me so easy.

TIMEOUT

....

Should You Give Him a Freebie?

Masha Lopatova, the wife of NBA player Andrei Kirilenko, said in an ESPN interview once that she allows her husband one night a year to do whatever he wants with whomever he wants.

"Male athletes in this country are extremely attractive. They get chased by women. It's hard to resist. It's the way men are by nature. When I'm aware and I let him do it, it's not cheating."

Masha also said, "What's forbidden is always desirable. It's the same way raising children—if I tell my child, 'No pizza, no pizza, no pizza,' what does he want more than anything? Pizza!"

While I completely understand where Masha is coming from, I think this whole way of thinking is B.S.

I've always heard that men (and women) can have sex without emotion or attachment. I don't believe this. Humans are led by emotion, and who's to say that one one-night stand couldn't lead to more? Why even leave the door open for that to happen?

By letting your man have a "free pass," you're opening the floodgates. One night a year? Then what

about the other nights he doesn't tell you about? Because, trust me, there will be other nights.

If you really think your man is going to stick to just one, you're fooling yourself. You're better off saying you're into swinging and swapping and into the group thing than saying you're cool with him being with someone else for even one night.

I get it. Men cheat. And this could be a way of dealing with that reality. But I'm not down with just handing my man some condoms with a pat on the back and letting him think it's okay. I know it may sound cool to be the kind of woman who would allow her man a one-night free pass. But then I have to ask, how much do you really value your relationship? Either I am enough for him, or I'm not.

If I'm not, then let's talk about that and go our separate ways.

I don't want to be with somebody who feels he needs more.

CHAPTER FOURTEEN

Ejection:
"He Cheated. Now What?"

Ejection: One of several disqualifying actions assessed to a player or coach by a game official, usually for unsportsmanlike conduct. Usually, a warning is given to the offender before he is actually ejected. When the offender is ejected, he must leave the immediate playing area or, in extreme cases, leave the stadium grounds.

Dice always asks, "Are you really meant to be with just one person for the rest of your life?"

Who knows? But I'm living this life and we'll see.

She's also always said, "Everybody cheats!"

When I ask her to clarify that, she says that everyone

has cheated at some point in his or her life. It could be with a boyfriend. It doesn't have to be in a marriage. We've asked a lot of people, and this has held true. It has sparked debate and heated arguments, but eventually people have to admit that they have cheated at least once in their lives—whether it was on a high school summer boyfriend or girlfriend or a husband or wife.

She says she doesn't believe it's possible for a person to go through his or her entire life and not cheat. I tend to agree with her. I'm not 100 percent in agreement with this, but I'm leaning in that direction.

So . . . what do you do if you find out you've been cheated on? It may feel good to go after the other woman. But you're not in a relationship with her. She may be foul, especially if she knows your man is married or in a relationship, but getting into it with her isn't addressing your problem. Your purpose in life isn't to teach her a lesson. And you will end up looking silly. Because, after all, she's not your problem. She has no obligation to not sleep with him. That's *his* responsibility.

You have to hold your partner accountable. You have to see things the way they are, not the way you want them to be. He participated. You're not with her—you're with him.

You have two choices if your man has cheated: leave or stay.

If you stay, then you have to forgive him. You can't harp on it and bring it up every five minutes and hold it over him. If you decide to stay, you have to make the best of it. Reboot, start over, and make it fresh and new.

If you eject him off your squad and decide to leave, don't cry wolf. Don't say, "I'm leaving!" and then not leave. Every single time you do that, your power diminishes. Then you become the doormat that will put up with anything. You are always talking about leaving. But you never do. So he knows it's only talk.

My dad told me this, and it stuck with me: "Be careful with shock value. The only person you end up shocking is yourself."

Don't jump up talking about you're outta there when you know in your heart you're not going anywhere. What happens when he says, "All right, go"? What will you do then? Stand there looking stupid? That was me when I was young. I liked attention, and I would be really dramatic, putting on a performance. I would storm out, hoping he'd run after me. I'd go to a friend's place, hoping he'd call and say he couldn't live without me. Then the call never came. And I ended up having to go back with my tail between my legs. And worse, he called my bluff and had carte blanche to do whatever he wanted.

If you're going to stay, stay without drama. But if you're going to leave, make a plan before your performance.

Know where you're going. Change your numbers (so you're not tempted when he actually does call in a week or two), don't leave a forwarding address, and don't look back.

You can leave and come back. But the leaving has to be real and longer than a day or two. You have to mean it. And you have to be resolved to never come back. I have seen relationships where the woman left, and he changed or something different happened and they got back together.

The only one that I can think of off the top of my head is Pink and Carey Hart. I don't know the details about why they broke up, but in 2008 they filed for divorce. After a couple of years apart, they got back together and even had a baby. And things seem to be going well. Carey told *People* magazine when they got back together: "We're rebuilding. Sometimes you have to take a couple of steps back to move forward."

Sometimes time apart helps one or both parties realize how much they miss and love the other person. You don't know what you have until it's gone. And sometimes people need to be reminded that the grass isn't always greener.

I love that Pink and Carey Hart were able to get back together. Most people would allow pride and their ego to get in the way of a reunion. It's easier to hold on to whatever broke you up than to pull out the tools and try to repair what's broken. So kudos to them and anyone else who is able to bring their family back together.

Note on leaving: It gets easier once you've done it. I know this from watching my mom. I know it must have been very hard for her to leave my dad. And while it took her a while to leave my stepdad, she finally did it and never looked back. She had nothing, but she knew she would be all right because she had done it the first time and landed on her feet.

Sometimes it takes you leaving to appreciate your relationship. If you have a lot of single friends, it's easy to look at how free they are and want that life back. But after a few weeks of partying and hanging out, you will realize that you miss your married life and your husband and all that goes with it. I don't recommend testing the waters just because. You should have a good reason to leave. But I just know that people are always looking over the fence, thinking someone else's life is better, more fun, more fulfilling.

But the truth is you have to work to make your life all of those things because there's really nothing new out there.

A friend of mine left when she found out her husband had cheated on her. She didn't intend to go back. But after a couple of months, she found she really didn't want to live without him. She loved him. But she didn't know if she could forgive him.

When she left, she fell into this single lifestyle with her friends, going to clubs. Guys were hitting on her and she said she felt dirty. And all she was thinking about was being with her husband. But she also couldn't shake that he cheated on her.

As the months went on, she missed him more than she was mad at him for cheating. At his core, he wasn't a dog. He was a good guy who made a mistake, so she decided to forgive him and go back. And they're doing great today.

"But . . . it will be a lot easier to leave if there's a next time," she told me. "And this time it will be for good."

Leaving the first time, you're going into the great unknown. It's scary. But if you leave again, you know what you're doing and where you're going and that you will survive, pick up the pieces, and make it.

I feel that relationships, especially marriage, should be sacred. You've committed to being with that person, and if you don't want to be with that person anymore you should let them know. Cheating is one of the most painful things a man can do to a woman because it renders her powerless. It makes a woman feel less than. And it forces her to make a decision about whether or not she's going to accept the behavior or walk away and move on.

So when I'm confronted with this question, I don't answer it the way I really feel, which is: "Get the fuck out of that relationship!" Because it's more complicated than that.

Here's what I do know: Just because a man has cheated, that doesn't make him a cheater. Things can happen. And while we'd like to think our man should always be in control of himself, the truth is sometimes he's not. I'm not making an excuse for why a man would cheat. I'm just saying that everything needs to be considered and all of the consequences to what you do next have to be weighed.

Just because he cheated doesn't mean he's a bad person. Good people do bad things all the time. And people do make mistakes.

(As I'm saying this, there's a huge voice inside still saying, "Fuck that!")

My friend Charlotte recently came to me because she found out that her boyfriend of three years had a one-night stand with this chick at the club after a basketball game (yes, he was an NBA player). She wanted to know what she should do.

The first thing I told her was to not go calling all of her friends and telling them what he did and throwing a big pity party. She will get a lot of people to attend, but when the pity party is over and she decides to stay with him (which she did), people will be looking at her as if she's crazy. Or worse, they will have a very negative opinion about him and she will have to now choose between her man and her friends and family.

This gets real tricky with family members because now your dude is sitting at family functions and everyone knows he cheated *and* you took his ass back. You both look lame. And trust me, everyone will have an opinion about your relationship. So my first piece of advice is to keep it tight. If you must confide in someone, limit it to that one person in your starting lineup of friends who is both wise and won't judge you later.

The next thing I told Charlotte was to do what she felt she needed to do. If she felt she needed to stay because that was what was best for her family, then she should stay and not worry about how it looked. If she couldn't live with the betrayal, then I understood that, too.

What I know is that every situation is unique and even cheaters are different from one another. Is he a dog and is his cheating chronic? Is he disrespectful and embarrassing with his cheating? Or did he make a mistake and is working hard to get you to forgive him? Is he trying to make changes?

You have to weigh the good against the bad. If the good outweighs the bad, then maybe you should stay. Maybe. Because here's the other truth: Sometimes you just can't forgive and forget. Sometimes the feeling of what he did is so painful that you simply can't see him the way you used to or you don't love him the same way. And once that happens, it's hard to come back.

Maybe you just need a break—at least a temporary one—to see if you can live without him.

Another piece of advice I've gotten from my mom is to never say never.

I remember being young and telling my mother, "I'm

never staying with a man who cheats on me. Period. End of discussion!" I was adamant about it.

"Never say never!" my mother would say, shaking her head.

Of course, she was right. My first love cheated on me . . . and even had a child (or maybe two) while we were in a relationship. And after that I vowed never again! I'm a little hardheaded, I guess.

I was the kind of person who had a lot of rules and lines in the sand in my life. I had determined what I would and would not put up with from an early age and decided I would stick by my guns, no matter what.

And while I was madly in love and even let him creep back in, when he showed his true colors, he was gone for good. I'm one to let a man know up front what I expect and that's that. If he messes up, I'm gone. My mother used to shake her head when she'd hear me say, "I'd never stay with a man who cheats on me."

Her response was, "Live a little and then get back to me on that."

What my mother knew is that "never" is a very long time. And "never" doesn't take into account extenuating circumstances. As a general rule, if a man cheats on you, you should leave him because a man who cheats is a cheater and it probably won't be the last time. And who wants to be in a relationship with someone who is a cheater?

But . . .

What if you really love that man and he really loves you and while he did do something that violated your relationship, what if it was a one-time thing? Should you throw away your entire relationship for a one-time mistake?

Only you can answer that question. And when I've been confronted on several occasions with this issue from friends, that's what I ask them: Can you live without him? Can you live with him knowing he was with someone else?

For me, I know it would eat at me. It did eat at me. It's a hard thing to just move on from a relationship. But it's not impossible. As far as I'm concerned, staying with him gives the man the upper hand. Remember, this is a game and if you want to win you always need to have the upper hand.

But what if in staying you find a way to turn it to your advantage? I know quite a few women who have been cheated on, unfortunately, and yet they stayed. They make their mate pay by spending his money and getting away with crazy things. A couple of my girls have even "gotten him back" by cheating on him.

That's all very messy to me. If your sole purpose is revenge or punishing him, then you're totally out of the game. Because while you're doing that, you're also destroying any chance you have of repairing the relationship. What's the point in that? Where's the love? And where can you grow if you're spending time being vengeful?

Life has taught me that sometimes you have to reevaluate your lines in the sand.

My approach is to shut it down. Just as I left Washington, D.C., when I had had enough of Doug's mess. I found out that leaving for a period of time is very effective—especially if you're leaving for real. No contact, no back-and-forth, no arguing and complaining. Just be gone.

Leaving gives you time to think and connect with what it is that will ultimately make you happen. In this case, I do believe the old adage "Time heals all wounds."

My mother was right about living a little. Time and age give you a totally different perspective on things. What I would "never" put up with in my twenties, I've softened a bit about in my thirties. Life has taught me that sometimes you have to reevaluate your lines in the sand.

I've had to adjust my lines quite a few times. One of the first things I shifted on was dating an athlete. I said I would NEVER date an athlete. Until Melo, anytime a basketball player or any athlete approached me, I would roll my eyes and keep it moving. He didn't stand a chance.

Then I met Melo and I had to move that line in the sand from "never" to "just this once."

Another one of my personal lines was having a baby out of wedlock. I would die before I had a baby without being married. Well . . . I had Kiyan, and he was three years old before we actually got married.

So I stopped saying what I would never do. I still have a few things that I believe will be deal breakers—like him having a baby with someone else while married to me—but honestly, you really don't know what you will do until you're confronted with the situation.

What I do know is that whatever decision you make, whether to leave or to stay, it should be *your* decision. And it should be based on what makes you happy.

How do you prevent your man from cheating? You can't. But what you can do is not let the relationship get stale. Don't give him a reason or an excuse to go out there. Sometimes we do that. Sometimes we get in a rut in a relationship, and it gets boring and routine or hectic and tense.

My husband and I spend a lot of time apart. Sometimes there's too much time apart. I used to think it was great because when we'd see each other it would be like a honeymoon. I had to reevaluate our situation and decide that the time apart was too much. Absence makes the heart grow fonder, they say. But out of sight, out of mind, too.

Realizing this, I won't let us go more than a week without checking in. If one of us has to hop on a plane for one day, then that's what we'll do. You have to look at your relationship honestly and see if there are some things you can do to keep it spicy. And make sure you're not slacking off in any area. (Not that a man needs a reason to cheat, because he doesn't. But you want to do all you can to make sure he doesn't have room to even think about it.)

If you feel like you've done everything right, then it's time to look more closely at him and decide if he's the kind of man you want to spend the rest of your life with. Some people just cheat to cheat. But if someone cheats and feels like he had some valid points, then you should listen and be honest with yourself.

Now don't get me wrong; women do cheat too. But for the most part when a woman cheats it's not because she's bored or she just saw some "hottie" that she has to get with. There are women who love sex and variety and all that comes with it—just as men do. But those women aren't generally the marrying type. If a woman who is married or in a committed relationship cheats, it's usually because there's something emotional missing from her relationship. It's a connection and a love that she's looking for that she's not getting at home. There tends to be so much more there when a woman like that cheats, which may make it harder for that relationship to survive.

CHAPTER FIFTEEN

Looking for a Trade: The Grass Is Not Necessarily Greener

Trade: In professional sports, a transaction involving an exchange of players' contracts or draft picks between teams. Typically trades are completed between two teams, but there are instances where trades involve three or more teams.

People look at my life with envy. I feel it. I even hear it. "How did *she* end up with him?"

People see the clothes, the cars, the money, the lifestyle, but that's all they see. Now, don't get me wrong. I feel blessed to live this life. But there's a whole spectrum that people rarely get to see. You see the lifestyle of the rich and famous, but you don't see the day-to-day drama and stress. You don't see the loneliness, the doubt, and the pain.

I rarely get to see my husband during the season. And if there is a FIBA World Championship or it's an Olympic year, I don't get to see him much when the season ends, either. There are eighty-plus games a season, and he's on the road for half of them. When he's not on the road, he's practicing or getting ready for a game or he's tired.

Of course, I get to go to the games. And, yes, I get really great seats to the games. But after ten years, sitting courtside at a basketball game is not a highlight of my life. In the beginning it was exciting, but not so much anymore. What I enjoy now is being home with my husband and my son or hanging with my friends and family.

Having a relationship in the public eye is so much more difficult. In 2012, Melo and I had some difficulties in our relationship that ended up on the cover of newspapers and on blogs. It was hard enough for just us to deal with it, but we had the added pressure of being bombarded with questions from the media about our relationship. Imagine that. Imagine every time you and your man have trouble, people are following you with cameras and microphones trying to get to the bottom of it before you two have even had a chance to do that.

While one in two regular marriages ends in divorce, the stats for celebrity marriages are much worse. When you see a Denzel Washington or a Samuel Jackson, who have both been married more than twenty years to their wives, you know how rare that is. I can't name ten Hollywood or celebrity couples that have been married only to each other and are still married. That's a shame. But I understand.

Aside from the temptations of people throwing themselves at your man or you, trying to break up your relationship, you can't have a normal life where your problems can simply be worked out quietly and privately.

I have a friend who was in a very public relationship with a man who dogged her out. They were both well known. She wanted to forgive him and stay, but it was so embarrassing and disrespectful that she left him. She loved him and still does, but the public scrutiny was just too much. How sad.

I know firsthand how things can get blown way out of proportion. During basketball season in 2012, my relationship landed on the front pages of just about every major newspaper in the country.

My phone rang at five in the morning. I almost didn't answer it, but it was my girl Po.

"Yo, La, you're on the front page of the *New York Daily News!*"

I was still a little sleepy and didn't think I heard her clearly.

"What?"

"You're on the front page for some shit Kevin Garnett said about you!"

The night before, I'd been at the game in Madison Square Garden between the Knicks and the Boston Celtics, and Melo and Kevin had gotten into something on the court. After the game, Melo waited for Kevin at the Boston team bus to let him know how he felt about whatever went down on the court. Melo ended up getting suspended for one game for doing that.

I did notice during the game that Melo and Kevin were jawing a lot at each other. But that's basketball, the heat of the game, and all that. I really didn't think anything of it. But when Melo went to have words with him, I knew it had to be more than an in-game beef. I asked Melo about it and all he said was that Kevin said things you shouldn't say to a person you have a friendship with or respect for. That's all he would say.

"I told him I'm not some rookie. We've been in this league a while together so don't treat me the way you'd treat a rookie." I'm sure the words were a little stronger than that, but that was the gist of what Melo said back to Kevin.

The next day, I'm on the cover of not one but several daily newspapers AND I'm smack-dab in the middle of what seemed to be some international scandal that involved a General Mills cereal. It was reported that Kevin had said to Melo that I tasted like Honey Nut Cheerios. How ridiculous! And now the media circus around it was surreal.

At first, I was embarrassed and angry, but then I just had to laugh about it. I mean, that was the most ridiculous thing I had ever heard, and if Kevin Garnett had actually said that about me, what exactly did it mean? Because he and I were never more than passing acquaintances. It was just dumb.

I wasn't ever going to bring up the Honey Nut Cheerios incident again. I was going to let my tweet be the final say on the matter. But since I'm writing this book, I might as well set the record straight for good.

Kevin Garnett in fact had never said that I tasted like Honey Nut Cheerios, as had been reported. I tried to figure out how this big lie was turned into a media firestorm. I still can't answer that one.

I finally made a joke of it and went on Twitter and said: "Not for nothing, but we ALL deserve a check or some free cereal 4all the publicity we've given Honey Nut Cheerios! LOL #cantbelieveeverything."

After a few weeks, it all died down (not before it turned into a whole story about how my relationship with Melo was on the rocks—more on that later). It still comes up every now and then, like every time New York plays Boston. Melo and Kevin are cool today. And now it's nothing but a faint memory.

The lesson is not to let things get to you. While I'm sure very few people will be in a position to have their lives and relationship on display for millions of people to comment on and have opinions about, there is some level of this in everyone's life.

Maybe your man did something embarrassing that your family won't let you live down. Maybe you did something that you regret. Maybe there's just some rumor about your relationship and no matter how hard you try to deny it, no one believes you. Maybe the rumors are true and you just want them to go away.

I guarantee you that while you may not end up on the front page with your image superimposed on a box of Honey Nut Cheerios, you will find yourself in an awkward position at least once in your relationship or your life, and you will simply have to deal with it. I suggest you do so with humor. Because eventually it will all fade away if you don't fuel it and give it power.

This wasn't the first embarrassing moment that I've had to endure in my life; it was just the most public. But I was able to get through it because of something my father used to always say to me growing up—"live your life inside out."

"Don't worry about what people think about you," he would say. "All you need to worry about is what you think about yourself."

That was the best advice, and I cling to it to this day. I

have to remind myself who I am. These people don't know me, so how can they really touch me? Why would I give them power over my life to make me sad or unhappy for one minute? If I live my life from the inside out, what happens on the outside can never touch my core. It can never alter my being.

It's very easy to get your feelings hurt and get sucked into the drama when you're on the other side of the rumors. But you can't control the rumors. I've seen false rumors of celebrities that spread so quickly on social media and ended up in the mainstream news. You can't control what they say about you; the only thing you can control in this equation is you.

How you carry yourself also matters. While people had a lot of fun with the whole Honey Nut Cheerios thing, the truth is they couldn't really take it much further than that because of how I carry myself. Of course, people make up total lies, but those lies fizzle when you have a track record of carrying yourself with respect.

I went on a 60 Day Challenge with rapper the Game. I saw what he was doing on Instagram and reached out to him to see what this program was all about. I wanted to get in better shape, and the program looked appealing. When I ended up taking the challenge, I would spend long days working out with the Game and we became friends. Our children now hang out together on playdates.

You've never heard one person say anything crazy

about Game and me because there is nothing crazy to report. That hasn't stopped folks from making up shit in the past. But there is this respect there. I'm not known as that chick that is loose. I have never been a serial dater and I don't have a track record for running through men. I have had male friends my entire life. I have close male friends who also happen to be famous, like Ludacris, but I've never been romantically linked to them—not even on sites that link any two people who happen to be standing next to each other.

You set the precedents for how people view you. But more importantly, knowing who you are inside and developing who you are inside and loving who you are inside makes whatever anyone says about you much easier to deal with.

TIMEOUT

....

Opposites Attract, and Complete

The best relationships are those that bring out the best in you. You don't get with a man to complete you. But he should certainly enhance your best qualities and help you work through becoming a better person. He should be there to hold you up, not tear you down. And he should be someone that you can learn from, and vice versa. I found that in Carmelo.

Melo's name suits him so well. He's just a very mellow person. It takes a lot to upset him. He's not the guy who unravels and screams and loses his cool. Sometimes you have to pry him just to open up. I'm just the opposite. I love to talk and I make friends fast. He takes a while to warm up to people, to trust them and let them in.

I have a bunch of friends and love to go out. He's more of a homebody and would prefer to stay home and watch a movie. He's an old soul who loves old music, cigars, and fine wine. I'm a big kid who loves to play.

We are definitely opposites in many ways. But that's part of the appeal. And our differences have brought good elements to each other's life. We all have

heard that opposites attract, but in relationships you have to make sure that you don't criticize or come down on your partner for being different. It's okay if he thinks differently, moves differently, or does things differently. Learn to learn from the differences.

I learned from Melo to be a bit more guarded. He doesn't worry about people knowing his business or having to deal with the heartbreak of friends betraying him because he doesn't let people in so easily. He has to really know and trust you to let you in. I'm learning from Melo to wait and watch people more before letting them in.

Of course, Melo has picked up some positive new habits from me, too. He has learned to hang out more and try things he wouldn't normally try. When I met him, he had never tried sushi. He thought he would hate it. But I didn't ridicule him and make him feel silly for not even trying it. I got him to try a California roll, which is made from avocado, cooked crabmeat, cucumber, and rice in a roll. Then I got him to try shrimp tempura. You have to introduce people to new things slowly. You can't be overbearing or hit them over the head with it.

Melo ate the cooked "sushi" for a month before he finally tasted a salmon roll and liked it. He now eats sushi and loves it!

Melo has gotten me to relax about a lot of things.

I'll be complaining about something someone wrote about me in the media and I'll say, "I'm not like that at all . . ."

And he'll say, "I know you're not like that. But more importantly, you know you're not like that, so why does it matter what anyone else thinks? Why do you care so much?"

I don't have an answer. And just like that, I get over it.

Melo turned out to be the best partner for me. Being with someone who is so different from me balances me out. He taught me that everything is not the end of the world.

"Whatever is going to happen will happen" is his philosophy. "Stressing about it is not going to change it."

That's really true. I've been that girl who takes things so seriously. So while opposites attract, it's more important that you have a mate you can learn something from and who can help you grow.

I'm grateful to have what I know is my perfect match. I've been through enough relationships that weren't good for me. When a relationship is right, a partner's differences can help strengthen your weaknesses. When it's wrong, it can totally tear you down.

OVERTIME

Baby Mama Drama

"What About the Kids?"

I was fortunate that I didn't have a baby's mom in my relationship with Melo. I'm not sure if I would have even entertained being with him if he had had a child and a baby's mom to deal with.

Realistically speaking, though, it's rare to run into a man these days who doesn't have children. And I must admit it does present a unique set of challenges.

For one, his baby's mother. She is someone who obviously was connected to your man long enough to produce a child. And they will forever be connected through that child. What kind of woman is she? Is she someone who still holds out hope that they can get back together one day and so she's just biding her time? Is she someone who will try to sabotage your relationship to get back with him? Or is she a mature woman who has moved on with her life and wants her child to have a relationship with his or her father?

The last kind of situation is rare. Very rare. Too many women today use their children as weapons or tools. They use visitation, child support, birthdays, and

holidays to get vengeance on their ex or try to curry favor with him.

You may want to get into it with her, and you may be absolutely right. But you can't win trying to play this particular game. Your only move is to check your man and tell him what you will and will not put up with from the very beginning. This is not a conversation to have in the middle of the drama. You have it at the very beginning of the relationship, before there's any sign of drama, when you're both calm and very much in love.

After you've told him how you expect him to handle his baby's mother, then step back and let him handle it. If he doesn't handle it and allows his baby's mother to control the entire game, it may be time for you to make a trade.

If your man doesn't establish the order of things—you first and his baby's mother second—then you will have problems throughout your relationship. Trade him.

The relationship that your man has with his children is a whole other thing. That's an important bond to foster. But the baby's mother should not be allowed to set the rules of engagement.

If dealing with a baby's mother isn't bad enough, what about having your man cheat on you and have a baby with another woman? Can you say "ultimate deal

breaker"? That would be it for me. (But remember, never say never).

This is a reality for a lot of women today as well. It's commendable that these women would take the "outside" kids and blend them into their family under those circumstances. I don't think I could do that. But I commend it.

It's not the kids' fault. They didn't ask to be involved in this drama. So everyone should put the needs of the children first. If you do agree to stay with your man after he's done the unthinkable, then you have to put all the anger and bitterness behind you as it pertains to the kids. If you made a decision to stay with him, that means you stay with all of the bullshit that goes with it. That means you love his kids, because those kids are siblings to your kids.

Daddy Drama

I had a friend named Debra who worked at one of the radio stations I worked at. She wanted to become a nurse. She decided to move back to her hometown somewhere in the Midwest to go to nursing school. She could stay with her family. And for an in-state student, the tuition would be cheaper. While there, she also got a job at a local radio station. Today, there are major radio conglomerates with stations in just about

every city. So she worked for an affiliate of the station we worked at together.

While at the radio station, she met a guy who was a deejay there. And slowly, she and I started to lose contact. Right after she moved, we talked just about every day. When she started dating this guy, we just lost touch. The next time I heard from her was several months later. She called to tell me she was pregnant. And she wasn't happy. I could hear it immediately. Debra was someone who could literally light up a room with her personality. She was the life of the party. And when we talked it was always a bunch of laughs and fun times. But whenever we talked after she got hooked up with this guy, she just sounded down and depressed.

I had heard that she wasn't doing well from some of our other friends, and she had also disconnected from them. We were trying to piece it all together. Finally, one day she shows up on my doorstep with her child and tears running down her face.

Of course I invited her to stay with me until she could figure it all out. This guy had not just cheated on her. He had given her an STD—actually a couple of STDs. This had been going on for a while, but she was so embarrassed that she couldn't pick up the phone and talk to anyone about it.

Note: Men who abuse—cheating and giving your woman a couple of STDs is considered abuse in my book—one of the first things they try to do is alienate you from your friends and family. They don't want you to have anywhere to run to or anyone who might actually talk some sense into you. They want you alone, scared, and feeling empty so they can do whatever they want without being checked.

But when Debra finally got fed up, she was gone. She sold all her furniture on Craigslist for ridiculous bargain-basement prices, she got a plane ticket, and she flew back to where she had friends and other family members. When I opened my door and saw her standing there, I just gave her a huge hug and told her I'd missed her.

She went from going to nursing school and becoming a nurse to having nothing and starting over again. I had been there. But thank God, I didn't have a child at the time.

Every day she was staying with me her little boy kept asking for his daddy. It was so sad to hear. And while I totally knew what Debra was feeling about that man, I also was heartbroken that she somehow had to figure out how to sever all ties with him yet allow him to maintain a relationship with his son. Every time her little boy would say, "Mommy, when's Daddy coming?" she felt guilty. He was too young to under-

stand what was going on. All he knew was that Daddy, who would normally be there to tuck him in or whatever, wasn't there.

I try not to think about it, but I do. What if Melo and I broke up and he remarried or got with someone else? How would I feel about this woman being in my son's life? These are modern issues. But my only advice is this: Be the mature woman. And put your child first. If that man is a good father, don't deny him the right to continue to be a good father. You divorced him, or vice versa, but he didn't divorce your child or children. You have to make it easy for him to be Daddy.

DOUBLE OVERTIME

A Message for Kiyan

There's really no manual on how to raise a kid. You do the best you can. And there's definitely no manual on how to raise your boy to be a good man. But I do know a few things that I have learned over the years about how to raise a child who is happy and generally a good person.

First, it starts with instilling in your child that happiness comes from within. Things cannot make you happy. People cannot make you happy. You have to find happiness within yourself.

I encourage my son, Kiyan, to be a leader, not a follower. For months he was into Spider-Man and he had this Spider-Man jacket that he wore to school every day. One day he stopped wearing it.

"Why aren't you wearing your Spider-Man jacket?" I asked him.

"Billy said he didn't like Spider-Man," he said.

"So because one of your friends doesn't like Spider-Man, you're not wearing your jacket? But *you* still like Spider-Man, don't you?"

"Yes," he said.

"Then you wear what you like. Don't stop doing

what you like because someone else doesn't like it. It doesn't matter what anyone else thinks."

I constantly reinforce the idea of following your heart and being true to yourself with him because kids are impressionable and they want to be liked, so they may follow the crowd. But I want him to know that he has to do what makes *him* happy. Not everyone is going to like it and not everyone is going to like him. But that's okay. Because his dad and I love him.

I have a greater challenge in this area because kids will like or not like Kiyan based not on who he is but on who his parents are. Especially in New York.

He came home one afternoon and asked me, "Mom, why do they hate Dad?"

"Who?"

"Some kids at school said, 'Your dad sucks!'"

The Knicks had had a tough loss the night before and I'm sure the parents of the kids must have voiced some opinion about the team and Melo and the kids picked it up and came to school with it. The average kid would never have to deal with that. And it goes the other way, too. A lot of people worship the ground Melo walks on, and Kiyan gets preferential treatment as a result. I try to keep him grounded either way.

I explain to him about how some people are really into sports and they get passionate about their team and when Daddy's team doesn't win, they are sad. It's not

personal. They don't really hate Daddy; they just want his team to win so badly, they get mad when the team loses. For a six-year-old it's hard to grasp. But I just let him know that they don't really hate his dad; it's just sports. And they don't really hate him, either. And if kids say mean things, he should just stay away from them.

I sometimes imagine what Kiyan's life must be like. We're living it, but for a kid born into a home where his dad is an NBA superstar whose face is on billboards in Times Square, and his mom is also on TV, it has to be surreal. When we go out, people run to get his dad's autograph and they are clamoring for a picture. I can't imagine what that must feel like to watch and live through, to see people wearing jerseys with your dad's name on the back. It's hard to know if your friends are friends because of who your dad is or if they genuinely like you for you.

That's why we named him Kiyan. We toyed with naming him Carmelo, but we didn't want him to have to carry the burden of his father's name. His name is Kiyan Carmelo Anthony. All the love goes out to the juniors of the world. But Melo and I both agreed that's a lot to put on a kid. There are certain expectations that go along with those names. What if Kiyan doesn't play basketball as well as his dad? What if he does? He will always be compared to Carmelo Anthony instead of being viewed on his own merits.

well behaved and well mannered he is. I can remember my mom and dad both saying the same thing about my brother and me. They would tell us how proud they were when they would run into someone who had seen us and that person would tell them how well mannered we were. More than anything, that's a true reflection of your parenting.

I drill into Kiyan to always say "please" and "thank you." I know it seems like common sense, but I'm amazed at how many kids don't have basic manners. That's unacceptable in our home. I stay on Kiyan about his manners. I also have to remind him to look people in the eye when they speak to him. Kiyan is shy and it takes a while for him to warm up. But when people meet him, he still must acknowledge them and look them in the face and say hello. I know he wants to run away or hide because he's so shy initially. But that comes off as rude. So I walk a fine line with him. He must say hello, he must be polite, and then he can run off to his room and hide afterward.

The other thing that I drill into him is that money doesn't grow on trees. We can afford to give him just about anything he wants in the world. But we don't. I don't believe that kids should ever feel like they can have everything. Money and things should never replace values.

And kids should be taught the value of money at a

We wanted him to be his own person. Judged on his own merits.

I always wanted a boy. I would never say it out loud. When people would ask me what I wanted, of course, I would say, "I don't care what I have as long as the baby is healthy." And that was definitely true. But deep down, I wanted a boy. The mother-son bond is such a strong one. I always imagined a son looking out for his mom, from his younger years through his adult years.

The other reason why I was so excited about having a son was because I'm a tomboy. I've never been a girlie girl. I play video games; I play basketball. I was always more comfortable doing that than playing with dolls and playing dress-up. I knew I could have that kind of fun with my son, and we do.

But having a son, I also feel a greater responsibility to make sure he has all the tools he needs to become a great person—not just a good man. For a mother, the goal isn't to prepare him for a relationship. The goal is to prepare him for life. If I can instill certain qualities, values, and morals in Kiyan, he will become a great mate down the road because he'll be a great person first.

One of the biggest compliments I get is when Kiyan stays over at a friend's house or has a playdate with a schoolmate and his friend's parents tell me h

young age. I believe that no matter what their family's economic status is, children should learn to respect money and understand the work that goes into getting it. I tell Kiyan that whatever Mommy and Daddy have and whatever we're able to provide for him, it's because we work extremely hard to get it. And we have to continue to work to have those things.

When we go into a toy store, he wants everything he sees. I tell him, "No, you get just one toy." We have to keep him grounded and humble. And again, I realize his life isn't normal. He is definitely exposed to more than the average kid and probably has more. But it's up to us to manage that. Kiyan has been asking for a dog for quite some time. I explained to him that we can't have a dog because we live in an apartment. And he reasons that we can take the dog to L.A. (He has a plan for everything.) He says he saw Kevin Hart take his dog on a plane. He saw it in some magazine.

"Kevin Hart has a private plane," I explained to him. "The rules are different there."

"Well, doesn't Daddy have a private plane?"

I told him no. "Private planes are expensive. And when we fly on one, it's a special privilege. That's not normal. And that's not our everyday life."

He was playing a video game on his iPad and there was a point at which he could get extra lives or get to another level, but it cost twenty dollars.

"Twenty dollars?! Absolutely not," I told him. "That's too much money."

He thought about it and came back and pulled out his little New York Knicks wallet and said, "If I give you twenty dollars, can I download this?"

I smiled inside. And I let him do it. He understood that if he wanted it, he'd have to pay for it and he figured it out, which I thought was cool. He's only six, but he understood that Mommy and Daddy aren't just going to give him what he wants and that he will have to sometimes earn it or buy it for himself. There's a cost to everything.

His lifestyle gives him access. But it's up to us to set the boundaries.

I will tell him he can't get something because it's too expensive. I need him not to expect things and not to think there is an endless supply of money. I make it a point. So he does understand the value of money.

The most important thing I think any parent must do for his or her child is to lead by example. Kids are sponges; they watch you and they soak up everything you do. You can tell your child to be nice to people, but if you're not nice to people, your child is going to watch what you do, not what you say. If you want your son to know how to treat a woman like a lady and be

a gentleman, he has to see his mom treated like a lady. He has to see the behavior.

I tell Kiyan that he has to be nice to little girls, and share and be kind. If he's playing rough, I say to him, "You wouldn't want anyone to be disrespectful to Mommy, would you? You wouldn't want anyone to be mean to Mommy, right?" I know he loves me, and when I put it like that, he gets it. But more than that, what he sees from day to day is his daddy treating his mommy like a lady.

Kiyan has never seen his dad scream at me or curse at me or hit me. All he knows is a loving household. That was important for Melo and me, and it's something we discussed from the very beginning. No matter what he and I may be going through—and we've had our moments—we don't expose Kiyan to it. We handle our adult business in private, and when we're around Kiyan, what he sees is love, family, and togetherness. If we're having an argument, why put him in the middle of it? That's something we have to work out. What we owe him is love and security.

I can tell a mile away a man who has a good relationship with his mom. There's a gentleness to a man in how he handles a woman when he has a solid relationship with his own mother. It's not just about whether

he opens the door or pulls out a chair; those are things any man can learn. But it's in the way he checks to make sure you're okay. And I'm not saying that a man who doesn't have a good relationship with his mother can't learn how to relate well with women. It just takes more work.

So it's really important that the first relationship Kiyan has with a woman (with his mom) is healthy, loving, and gives him the perspective of how he should see all women in his future.

I never want to be that mom who thinks no woman is good enough for my son. You've seen that before. Or maybe you've been on the receiving end of a mother who didn't think you were good enough for her son. I think that actually reflects poorly on the mother.

I feel like if I raise my son to be his own man and to have good judgment and make good choices, then whoever he decides to be with, I'm cool with that. Even if I question his choice, I have to accept it and know that even if it doesn't work out, that's something he has to go through to learn. When you get involved and start voicing your opinion about his mate you can sometimes create a wedge between you and your son. Or worse, he'll probably stay in that relationship longer than he needs to just to prove a point. Or worse still, what if you're wrong? What if that person was the

right one and you badgered him to get out of that relationship and he ends up miserable?

My rule of thumb will be to stay out of his affairs of the heart (unless he asks for my opinion, and then I will tell him that I trust him to make the right choice).

I always want to respect my son's choices of women. And I think I'm teaching him well enough that he'll be able to make good choices.

But really, I don't even want to think about that. It's too soon. I want my son to enjoy being a kid. I want him to enjoy his childhood.

And now I'm still showing him how women want to be treated. I shower Kiyan with kisses and I tell him that I love him all the time.

I also know that in order for him to be complete and happy, he must have balance in his life. Mommy can be there with the love and affection, but he also needs it from Daddy.

Boys need their daddies. As much as women know about men and what it means to be a man, we're not men. You can be the best mom in the world, the best single mom. There's still a void. We don't know what it's like to be a man and what that embodies. That's the toughest part, teaching a man to be a man. I don't believe a woman can do it.

I can tell when a man I encounter is somebody who grew up around only women all the time—he's

different. I have seen big, burly football players who didn't have any man in their lives, and I could tell that by how they behaved, even how they talked.

Melo is very present in Kiyan's life. There are times when I need Melo to have certain conversations with Kiyan that I know would resonate differently coming from him. And it's not about disciplining Kiyan, because I find myself being a lot tougher than Melo is about certain things. I never threaten Kiyan with "Wait until your dad gets home," because I'm more of the disciplinarian than Melo is. He loves Kiyan so much, he lets him get away with a lot. But when it's time to have a talk with Kiyan about something and I'm not getting through, Melo does. Kiyan listens. It's just different.

I believe that when it comes to raising a son, you need a man around. You don't have to be married, and the man doesn't have to be your son's father, but there has to be a male figure in his life. Again, I applaud the single moms. But it's a whole lot easier if there's a man to lean on when you're raising a boy.

Melo's on the road a lot, so sometimes my brother steps in. Kiyan can be acting up and I'll say something and he may not listen. My brother will say, "Didn't you hear your mom say sit down?" And Kiyan will sit down.

That's not to say that a mom can't have authority.

For the most part, Kiyan does listen when I tell him to do something. But there is a way that men talk to boys that's just different and necessary.

While a woman can't teach a boy how to be a man, what a woman can do is teach him how to treat a woman. She can show him how important it is to be a gentleman and have manners and be grateful.

I'm raising a good man. And I hope everyone can find a good man. Beyond that, I hope that you find yourself first—be happy with who you are and be true to yourself. Because only when you're complete and happy can you truly enjoy that good man when he comes along.

FINAL BUZZER

It All Comes Back to You

As I share all of these stories and life experiences, I'm struck with one thought: No matter what happens, it still all comes back to you.

It will never really be about a man, looking for Mr. Right, or finding a man. Your journey, and the success of that journey, will always be about finding you. Finding what you like and don't like and not settling for less than what you deserve—whether it's a man, a job, your home, your friendships.

What I've learned through my various experiences is that no one can love me more than I love myself. So my job is to make sure that I do that to the best of my ability. Because when you truly love yourself is when you're open to having the best things in life come your way.

I think the universe knows it and that whole law of attraction thing is real.

Start with you and all these other things will be added layers to the love you already have for yourself.

ACKNOWLEDGMENTS

Thank you to my mom. You have equipped me with the skills, and more importantly with the love to make it through this journey called life. I couldn't imagine doing it without you. To my dad, thank you for showing me life is about living! Because of you, Dad, I know what loving myself from the inside out means.

To Mel, you've showed me what loving someone is truly about. Ten years and counting, and I still get butterflies in my stomach every time I see you. To Kiyan, I thank GOD every single day for blessing me with you. I know what it feels like to love someone more than myself. There is nothing I wouldn't do for you.

To my family and friends. Sometimes I ask myself what did I do so right in my life to be blessed with an army of people who have my back no matter what. Love you all from the bottom of my heart.

Acknowledgments

To my business team. None of this is possible without all the hard work you each put in. Just know how much I appreciate it and never take it for granted. Thank you so much!

Karen Hunter . . . we did it! Thanks for making my first writing experience such a great one. Couldn't have done it without you.